THE MAN WHO SHOT LIBERTY VALANCE

REEL WEST

ANDREW PATRICK NELSON, SERIES EDITOR

Reel West is a unique series of short, neatly packaged volumes exploring individual western films across the whole history of the canon, from early and classic westerns to revisionist and spaghetti westerns. The series considers the many themes and variations that have accrued over more than a century of this most American of film styles. Intended for general readers as well as for classroom use, these brief books will offer smart, incisive examinations of the aesthetic, cultural, experiential, and personal meaning and legacy of the films they discuss and will provide strong arguments for their importance—all filtered through the consciousness of writers of distinction from within the disciplines of film criticism, journalism, and literature.

Also available in the Reel West:

Broken Arrow by Angela Aleiss
Ride the High Country by Robert Nott
Thelma & Louise by Susan Kollin
Ride Lonesome by Kirk Ellis
Blood on the Moon by Alan K. Rode

THE MAN WHO SHOT LIBERTY VALANCE

CHRIS YOGERST

University of New Mexico Press • Albuquerque

Printed in the United States of America

ISBN 978-0-8263-6838-6 (paper)
ISBN 978-0-8263-6839-3 (ePub)

Library of Congress Cataloging-in-Publication data is on file with the Library of Congress.

Founded in 1889, the University of New Mexico sits on the traditional homelands of the Pueblo of Sandia. The original peoples of New Mexico—Pueblo, Navajo, and Apache—since time immemorial have deep connections to the land and have made significant contributions to the broader community statewide. We honor the land itself and those who remain stewards of this land throughout the generations and also acknowledge our committed relationship to Indigenous peoples. We gratefully recognize our history.

Cover photograph: still from *The Man Who Shot Liberty Valance*
Series design by Felicia Cedellos
Layout by Isaac Morris
Composed in Adabe Jenspn 9.5/13.75

CONTENTS

1. | When the Legend Becomes Fact

"When the legend becomes fact, print the legend."

These words, spoken by newspaper reporter Maxwell Scott (Carlton Young) near the end of the film *The Man Who Shot Liberty Valance,* may be the most consequential words uttered in film history. Scott has just learned that contrary to established lore, the bullet that killed the outlaw Liberty Valance (Lee Marvin) so many years ago did not, in fact, come from the gun of the idealistic Eastern lawyer Ransom Stoddard (James Stewart) but from the rifle of the rugged Westerner Tom Doniphon (John Wayne). Despite now-Senator Stoddard's self-deprecating and unimpeachable admission, the seasoned reporter knows that the scoop should never see the light of day. The truth, Scott well understands, would be no match for the wildly popular origin story of a now-celebrated and respected public figure. When Scott crumples his printed report, Stoddard asks if he intends not to publish it. "This is the West, Sir," Scott replies. "When the legend becomes fact, print the legend."

On the surface, *The Man Who Shot Liberty Valance* is about the fall of the Old West and rise of the twentieth century. Looking deeper, the film weighs the passage of time and how we collectively tell stories about the past. In the twenty-first century, we have seen a move from analog to digital technology, a similarly disparate distinction between the frontier to modern civilization. Our lives have been transformed during both transitions. *The Man Who Shot Liberty Valance* is a multilayered rumination on time, having both historical nostalgia and an understanding for the necessity of progress.

The idea of printing legends is important to the history of popular culture. Historians look at Hollywood memoirs with caution, akin to asking, "Are we getting the legend or the facts?" Stars love to print their own legends. For historians, getting the truth about the past requires us to play the role of Ranse, standing between the powers of the past looking for a path forward. Does the author (say, Jack Warner) have a reputation for weaving self-fulfilling tales or (like Bette Davis) a penchant for blunt honesty.

When I was researching my biography on the Warner brothers, I was perplexed by the tell-all memoir written by Lina Basquette, Sam Warner's wife. I asked historian Kevin Brownlow, who had come to know her, if she was trustworthy. He assured me that she tended toward the hyperbolic but was a trustworthy person in terms of the facts. As a historian, I've regularly found myself questioning legends. This is a large part of why this film has stuck with me for so long.

For a long time, I shied away from reading what others thought of *The Man Who Shot Liberty Valance*. This film had enough of an impact on my own work and intellectual growth that I didn't want to know other's opinions. This is the purest relationship one can have with a film, where seeing the film is completely fulfilling, where the viewer connects to every frame, each piece of dialogue. The film just works, as we might say. No doubt the combination of legendary talent in John Ford, John Wayne, Jimmy Stewart, Lee Marvin, and an impressive supporting cast had something to do with the film's longevity.

Figure 1. "The Man Who Shot Liberty Valance" title card

With its all-star cast, no other western connects such towering figures in a film with such deeply mythological implications. *The Man Who Shot Liberty Valance* is like *King Kong vs. Godzilla,* but with cowboy hats. The balance of the universe is at stake in both films, but on different terms, featuring the two major stars in opposition to one another. Ford could not have cast better stars to embody the tension between the frontier and the future of civilization. The big, tough Tom embodies the survival-of-the-fittest mentality of the Wild West. The lanky, cerebral Rans embodies the intellectualization of life that would civilize the modern world and bring the West into the next century. Rule by collective law is about to supersede rule by the dominant individual. Tom knows he is of a dying era. Ranse knows what the future will require. And through their combined fates, the lawless, frontier mentality of the Old West sacrifices itself for benefit of a new world where law will rule the land. From such perfect cinematic moments are legends made.

Although critics of the day may not have recognized the film's greatness, often deriding it as little more than a "horse opera," audiences knew a good thing when they saw it, and *Liberty Valance* became one of the most popular films of 1962. The film even established Wayne's iconic and sometimes mocked use of the word "pilgrim" (see *Full Metal Jacket*). This film connects to nearly every western that came before or after. Its focus on the mythology of the West—printing legends—allows the film to operate on a level above the rest in how it critiques not just a specific history but how history is made and disseminated to others. *The Man Who Shot Liberty Valance* offers us a framework to critique these other works in how they use history.

Every film that has tackled a turning point in civilization has been informed by Ford's 1962 masterwork. Some of the best filmmakers of subsequent generations were inspired by Ford. Martin Scorsese's *Goodfellas* gives us the legend of the modern gangster while adding harsh facts to offer a more complete story. Steven Spielberg's *Saving Private Ryan* upholds the legend of our Greatest Generation while offering the devastating reality that soldiers endured on our behalf. Both filmmakers openly and regularly praise Ford, their films often nodding to his work.

During this great film's sixtieth anniversary, *The Man Who Shot Liberty Valance* received a grand nod of approval in Spielberg's autobiographical flick *The Fablemans* (2022). In Spielberg's film, Sammy Fableman (whose life is based on the director's) gets a chance to meet John Ford in his office. This is a story that Spielberg himself has told numerous times and is also referenced in Joseph McBride's exhaustive Ford biography. Sammy experiences exactly that Spielberg has told us.

The kid sits in a waiting area surrounded by film posters, including *The Man Who Shot Liberty Valance*. When Ford allows him in, the director gives the kid a lesson on pinpointing the horizon in a painting. "If the horizon's at the bottom, it's interesting. If the horizon's at the top, it's interesting. If the horizon's in the middle, it's boring as shit. Now, good luck to you. And get the fuck out of my office." For those familiar with Ford or who have seen the director's cantankerous attitude to Peter Bogdanovich in *Directed by John Ford* (1971), the dialogue in this scene is easily plausible.

A HISTORY OF FLUCTUATING POPULARITY

In 1927, the *Exhibitors Herald* ran a study of northwestern and midwestern theater owners and found that westerns were their second overall choice for rentals. About a quarter of theaters chose westerns as the genre that gave them their best returns. Film Booking Offices of America (FBO, eventually merging into RKO) was primarily producing westerns, and their top star, Fred Thompson, was second in popularity only to Tom Mix.[1]

In the late 1920s, Fox was producing more westerns than any other genre. Of course, these were the days when John Ford was pioneering epic silent westerns like *The Iron Horse* (1924) and *3 Bad Men* (1926). The genre was popular, and the Wild West was a real memory for many still alive in the United States. Wyatt Earp even spent time in Tinseltown sharing legends of his days in Tombstone. Old timers who lived through the Wild West spun first-hand tales and legends, some if which Ford eventually turned into films.

As the United States was climbing out of the Great Depression in 1939, a *Motion Picture Herald* headline proclaimed, "Westerns on Way

Out as Public Taste Changes."[2] Most studios were "turning to melodramas" while some focused on "modernizing Westerns." Certainly, during a time of economic desperation, films that spoke to the moment most directly worked for studios like Warner Bros. Major western stars like Tom Mix went on to other careers. However, the downturn would not last, as by 1939, the genre would be revitalized by John Ford as he took John Wayne from the B-film treadmill by introducing him in an A-list production with *Stagecoach* (1939). The *Chicago Tribune* described the film as a "treat loaded with suspense" before predicting Wayne's ascension to major star "who will have feminine hearts doing handsprings."[3] The *New York Times* boasted how Ford "has a motion picture that sings a song of camera" as he "prefers the broadest canvas, the brightest colors, the widest brush and the boldest possible strokes."[4] The raves for not only *Stagecoach* but Ford's other 1939 western, *Drums Along the Mohawk*, prefigures what would be a massive explosion of western popular culture in film and, later, television for the next two decades.

The Wall Street Journal reported that in 1948, a quarter of Hollywood's output were westerns. "Filmland's cowpokes are dusting off their saddles and guitars," *The Wall Street Journal* reported, "and [they] are starting to gallop through the 100 sagebrush epics scheduled for shooting this year."[5] Producer Harry Sherman, who brought Hopalong Cassidy to the big screen, had produced 157 westerns up to that point and claimed that any of them costing up to $1.5 million were "as reliable as ham and eggs." The genre's reliability was based on three components: "action, putting the hero in physical jeopardy, and a chase."[6]

Many of the early westerns were popular among children, who often came to inexpensive daytime screenings. The B-film grindstone was perfect for those action-packed westerns. In fact, theaters in Los

Angeles that specialized in westerns reported that "the problem is how to get young patrons out of the theatre, not into it." Cap guns had to be checked at the box office because screenings turned into make-shift shootouts. Many of these low-budget films were shot in a series, with the same main actors, creating a universe of sorts that audiences would be familiar with. For example, John Wayne starred in a series of such films for Warner Bros. under producer Leon Schlesinger in the early 1930s.

Andre Bazin's *The Evolution of the Western* (1955) tracks the genre's more literary track throughout the 1950s.[7] Bazin acknowledges the genre's rebirth after being nearly nonexistent during World War II (John Ford and many others were off serving, of course). Films like *The Gunfighter* (1950), *The Naked Spur* (1953), and *Vera Cruz* (1954), for Bazin, build on the classic genre tropes of adventure to add more literary feelings, sensibilities, and lyricality to the story. Bazin summarizes his view of westerns as having "novelistic" characters, meaning that "without departing from the traditional themes they enrich them from within by the originality of their characters, their psychological flavor, and engaging individuality, which is what we expect from the hero of a novel."[8] Such characters perfectly prefigure the moral conflicts of *Liberty Valance*'s Ranse and Tom, both of whom understand that for the betterment of society, they must do something they don't want to do.

Nobody embodied the western hero more than John Wayne, who was the top star in Hollywood throughout the 1950s. The *Motion Picture Herald* billed Wayne as the "star of stars" in 1955.[9] Hollywood made fifty-four westerns in 1958 (roughly 28 percent of their output). Films like blacklist fable *High Noon*, John Ford's *The Searchers*, Howard Hawks's star-studded *Rio Bravo*, a range of Anthony Mann–directed westerns starring Jimmy Stewart, and George Stevens's epic films *Shane* and *Giant* all helped the western maintain top billing toward the end of the decade.

However, as that generation of stars and filmmakers retired or died, the popularity and cultural stature of the western began to decline. The genre that had been such a powerhouse for decades, like the superhero genre of today, had lost its appeal, and audiences, who were now oversaturated with westerns both on the big screen and on TV, were turning to other forms of cinematic entertainment. Despite a trend of revisionist westerns directed by auteur filmmakers that kept the genre engaging, its popularity was nothing compared to previous decades.

By the time *The Man Who Shot Liberty Valance* was released, television westerns had become ubiquitous. The 1950s saw multiple seasons of Roy Rodgers and Gene Autry series. Zane Grey had an anthology series. *Rawhide*, the show that introduced Clint Eastwood as a leading western hero, had begun its six-year run in 1959. And in 1962, when *The Man Who Shot Liberty Valance* hit the big screen, television audiences were sitting down to watch *The Virginian*, which would run for nearly a decade. The genre was so omnipresent that timing was perfect for a film that managed to comment on almost the entirety of the American frontier story.

The lack of Native American characters in *The Man Who Shot Liberty Valance* may raise eyebrows and is something Ford would remedy in his 1964 production of *Cheyanne Autumn*. Having Native Americans excluded from *The Man Who Shot Liberty Valance* tracks with the film's message about legends. Ford was nostalgic about the past, perhaps to a fault, and including Native Americans would have forced him to reckon with the treatment of Indigenous peoples on the frontier. Instead, the film is dedicated to maintaining the accepted American narrative and celebrating the legend of rugged individuals who kept order on the frontier. Of course, at the same time, Ford is lifting the veil by reminding us that behind every legend is the rest of the story.

2. | Mythologizing the West

When John L. O'Sullivan used the term *manifest destiny* in 1845, he did not realize that he had coined an expression that would define a movement, an era, and an eternal idea. It wasn't until other newspapers jumped on his catchphrase, originally published in the *Democratic Review*, that it came to highlight the perceived right to expansion assumed by the United States. Throughout the 1800s, the United States was expanding fast, from the Louisiana Purchase to the invasion of Florida that resulted in the Transcontinental Treaty. Seeking new boarders seemingly became the government's favorite pastime. During his 1893 address at the Wisconsin Historical Society, history professor Frederick Jackson Turner spoke of the continued pursuit of the frontier as a "perennial rebirth" that continued America's "touch with simplicity or primitive society" that defines "American character."[1] The famous "frontier thesis" was first presented as a scholarly paper presented at the American Historical Association (then the Organization of American Historians) during Chicago's 1893 World's Fair.

Turner described the frontier as "the meeting point between savagery and civilization" where the "wilderness masters the colonist."[2] Seeking the frontier builds character by stripping the civilized individual of progress and forcing them to get in touch with root forms of survival. Turner did more than wax nostalgic about the character-building escapades driven by manifest destiny. He also fully understood that these years were plagued with Indian Wars and Native American removal policies. It was also not simply the US Government's sense of endless empire that drove us west; individuals had their own reasons for setting out into the great unknown. Many were driven west by the promise of prosperity during the California Gold Rush. Others simply sought a better life over the horizon. As Turner observed, "The exploitation of the beasts took hunters and traders to the West, the exploitation of the grasses took the rancher west, and the exploitation of the virgin soil of the river valleys and prairies attracted the farmer."[3]

Turner defined the Westerner, the symbolic rugged individual, as one "with a grim energy and self-reliance [that] began to build up a society free from the dominance of ancient forms . . . who defended himself and resented governmental restrictions."[4] The American character was defined by the frontier and its associated mentality informed by freedom from structure. Turner argued that American democracy was borne "out of the forest, and it gained new strength each time it touched a new frontier."[5] Hence the identity crisis when the frontier closed. As the country coped with this new orientation, people like the character Tom Doniphon were forced to cope with their own fading identities as rugged bearers of community strength.

Turner's frontier thesis has long dominated conversations of the frontier and its Wild West sub-history. Contemporary notions of freedom and rugged individualism harken to Turner's analysis of the frontier, where, during a brief period, "the bonds of custom are broken and unrestraint is triumphant."[6] Understanding the American West via manifest destiny dominated popular culture for generations, ranging from Zane Grey's dime novels to Hollywood's films. *The Man Who Shot Liberty Valance* operates, through an extended flashback, at the end of the frontier as we collectively understood it. The common conception of frontier as a Wild West setting can largely be understood as the decades preceding 1890, at which time the US census determined that there was no longer an advancing frontier line.

The location of the frontier changes over time to fit the ideas and interests of a given era. For the frontier in cinema, locations range from across to globe to outer space—the final frontier. Historian Clyde Millner has argued that "the west has no set of external boundaries, it has no fixed geographic or cultural unity."[7] Because of this vast range of possibilities, the American West is something that almost anyone can imagine. When John Ford created his visions of the American West, Japanese director Akira Kurosawa utilized his own frontier interpretation for his samurai films. Sergio Leone utilized the American West in Italian westerns, taking the notable television actor Clint Eastwood and making him world famous as the man with no name in the *Dollars Trilogy*. George Lucas's *Star Wars* franchise is often labeled as a space western. In the twenty-first century, the western has become somewhat of a prestige undertaking exemplified in films like *The Power of the Dog* (2021). There have also been interesting horror-western mashups, such as *Ravenous* (1999), *Zombieland* (2009), and *Bone Tomahawk* (2015). Contemporary applications of the frontier mentality and rugged individualism persist in television shows like *Justified* and *Yellowstone*.

In her essay "Selling the Popular Myth," Anne M. Butler parallels the frontier's heroic mythos with the common interpretations of Davy

Crockett. The coonskin-capped frontiersman embodies "real and imagined events" that "captured important aspects of 'Americanness.'"[8] The folk hero stature of Crockett is unique in that what he really said, did, or thought matters less than his Westerner-frontiersman identity, a status that was cemented during his leadership in Texas during the revolution in 1836 and after his death at the battle of the Alamo Mission in San Antonio, which itself became a mythological locale of the American frontier.

As Butler points out, Crockett's "feats are tightly woven into the fabric of values that many Americans think they exhibit and cherish," such as "independence, honesty, fair play, self-reliance, loyalty, courage, justice, [and] love of freedom."[9] Of course, each of these buzzwords has been interpreted differently throughout history. For example, many people in the 1800s thought that relocating Native Americans to reservations was just. One's idea of justice—be it legal justice or frontier justice—depended on where one stood in North America.

The American West, as historian Dee Brown has described it, has become a clichéd model to examine the nation in both in its contemporary and historic forms. However, it was the "nameless settlers" who "put down roots," "believed in manifest destiny," and were driven by "Providence" to settle down on the frontier.[10] There is a point at which the frontier was conquered, the American West was settled, and the clock was ticking for those who felt most free on the frontier. *The Man Who Shot Liberty Valance* operates during this final transition period, when civilization was becoming the standard and laws were enforced. Although frontier justice may have lost its acceptability in the eyes of the law, it lingered in the American West as a necessary means during the region's fitful last years of settlement.

THE MAN WHO SHOT LIBERTY VALANCE AND THE HOLLYWOOD WESTERN

Acclaimed critic Robert Warshow, author of the 1954 essay "Movie Chronicle: The Westerner," explored the significance of the classic western that would be deconstructed years later in films like *The Man Who Shot Liberty Valance*. "The two most successful creations of American movies," Warshow claimed, "are the gangster and the Westerner: men with guns."[11] The traditional western hero, like the gangster, is a commanding and powerful man with a mythical presence who somehow manages to hold onto an element of reality. Western hero and gangster both derive their power from the end of a gun barrel, each feeling that he is doing what's right. Justified in their causes, the gangster and Westerner share many qualities. Yet while the Westerner traditionally rides off into the sunset, the gangster often dies alone in a hail of gunfire.[12]

Warshow explained that the western hero stands for some version of frontier justice and claims to fight to keep order; however, this will "never correspond exactly to his real motives; they only offer him his opportunity."[13] Without the need to continually defend justice, the Westerner would serve no purpose. He would just be another man in the town, drinking and brawling. He revels in his honor, which gives him a sense of invulnerability that is the source of his charisma. The Westerner remains relevant because he lives in the contemporary world, where he "presents an image of personal nobility that is still real for us."[14] Having one foot in reality and the other in myth is a primary reason why westerns work as social commentary. One can use the western to comment about gender inequality, American racism, the nature of violence, the moral ambiguity of a vigilante, the problem of a black-and-white view of right and wrong, or the necessity to understand order versus chaos. For example, *The Wild Bunch* (nature of violence), *Johnny Guitar* (inequality, parable for the blacklist), *Forty Guns* (role of gender in society), *Shane* (role of the gunfighter) and *The Searchers* (explores right and wrong as well as a view of Native Americans) each easily connect to the era in which they were produced.

Warshow saw the Westerner through one primary lens, that "he is a killer of men."[15] Many films, from George Steven's *Shane* (1954) to Clint Eastwood's *Unforgiven* (1991), tackle the uncomfortable reality that some of these heroes would not be heroes without bloodshed. Tom Doniphon's heroism is tied up in his ability to enact violence, to be the toughest guy "this side of the picketwire." To speak about many frontier heroes honestly would be to admit that they are driven by violence, regardless of which side of good and evil they are on. The Westerner's most important asset is his gun, though "it is not violence at all which is the point of the western movie, but a certain image of a man, a style, which expresses itself most clearly in violence."[16] It is the image of what a man looks like when participating in such action that is the attraction to him. Warshow tells us that "a hero is one that looks like a hero," as he recalls seeing boys play with guns imitating the heroes they see on TV and in comic books.[17] They are less concerned by the idea of hurting others and more focused on the image of toughness that the gun provides. It is this toughness that comes to be scrutinized as the genre evolved. John Wayne has always been a shining example of tough, rugged, frontier individualism.

The Man Who Shot Liberty Valance offers a critique about changing times. The western in the 1960s was nearing the end of its decades-long run as a major genre, while the culture in America and Hollywood was also changing. Movie studios were being bought out by conglomerates, the industry's founders were dying, and directors like John Ford, who had been in cinema since the beginning of the form, were nearing the ends of their careers. New audiences were coming to the movies, the biggest crowds since 1946, which meant demands for new stories and new stars—Steve McQueen, James Coburn, Yul Brenner, Eli Wallach, Robert Vaughn, and Charles Bronson. Movies continued to grow in popularity, but the number of productions was down significantly from the years when a Hollywood studio could crank out well over fifty films per year. *The Man Who Shot Liberty Valance* provided the genre a useful closing point from which new filmmakers could start afresh.

The Man Who Shot Liberty Valance perfectly incorporates standard genre tropes like rugged individualism, frontier town, and a lawless outlaw. The location, despite not using Monument Valley's stunning vistas, is standard frontier stuff. We have a carpentry/undertaker parlor, newspaper office, town's primary restaurant, a saloon, a ranch, and a convention hall. The film also incorporates poetic storytelling devices, many stemming from Dorothy Johnson's short story, such as the desert cactus rose and the silver knobbed bullwhip. These props signify the film's emotional struggle, which echoed the struggle of many communities during the death of the so-called Wild West and the encroaching progress of the future.

PRINTING THE LEGEND

The Man Who Shot Liberty Valance is a thought-provoking western that explores the contrast between law and lawlessness, showcasing the complex moral choices faced by its characters in the untamed frontier of the Old West. Operating between heroism and legend, the film raises questions about the importance of truth and the stories we tell to shape our history and culture.

As one of Ford's last westerns, *The Man Who Shot Liberty Valance* takes the conflict that had driven the genre to a logical conclusion. The film stars two actors famous for playing very different western heroes, John Wayne and Jimmy Stewart. Rans Stoddard (Stewart) is an aging US senator who goes back to the town of Shinbone, where he began his law career, to attend the funeral of an old friend, Tom Doniphon (Wayne). The clash between Stoddard and Doniphon is that of order and chaos, civilization and savagery, that had molded the genre to this point. Doniphon is the Westerner, the man with the gun who can kill to protect the newly civilized world. Stoddard is the man who is working to implement law, and Liberty Valance (Lee Marvin) is the constant savage threat to the New World. In the middle of it all is Hallie (Vera Miles), who begins the film as Doniphon's girl and ends it as Stoddard's wife.

Ford knew, as we all do, that the conflicts of the Wild West eventually came to an end. The West became civilized, and the real-life Westerner faded away. Each character in *The Man Who Shot Liberty Valance* is representative of America's path toward progress. Civilization (Stoddard) ultimately wins, but not without the help of the wilderness (Doniphon). The savage (Valance) became a fear of the past. Hallie and her cactus rose, a regular gift from Doniphon during their courtship, represent a level of uncertainty about the settled West and an element of nostalgia. When Doniphon dies, she picks cactus rose to place on his casket. Though she doesn't necessarily regret marrying Stoddard, just as America didn't regret becoming more civilized, Hallie knew, as they all did, that the old days were over. There was no place in the New World for the western hero, for he has been replaced by lawmakers.

The famous line near the end of the film speaks volumes. Upon finding out that Stoddard never actually shot Liberty Valance (an action that gained him the recognition that launched his career), a journalist says, "This is the West, sir. When the legend becomes fact, print the legend." *The Man Who Shot Liberty Valance* is, in the words of Thomas Schatz, "Ford's effort to print both the fact and the legend, both history and myth, and to suggest how the two interpenetrate one another."[18] The film explores the inevitable end of the Wild West, but as we see with Hallie, it is not without regret or remorse. There was something special about the Old West, as seen in Ford's earlier films. The frontier was an endless, hopeful place where possibilities were endless. The violent rule had to come to an end; the reality is that when the Westerner was no longer needed, he simply faded away. However, he does not die in the traditional sense. "Doniphon does not ride off into the sunset or across Monument Valley, but into the Valley of Death."[19] The iconic demise of Tom Doniphon is Ford's farewell to the hero he created with the Ringo Kid. *Stagecoach* and *The Man Who Shot Liberty Valance* are bookends of the most important period within the genre's history.

The Man Who Shot Liberty Valance explores themes of justice, morality, civilization, and the use of violence in establishing order in the Wild West. As Ransom becomes involved in local politics and attempts to bring law and order to Shinbone through peaceful means, he ultimately faces a moral dilemma (in addition to finding himself in a love triangle between Doniphon and Hallie). The film ultimately showcases the importance of myth and legend in the American West.

Depictions of rugged male individualism made Wayne a star and, in this film, are on the chopping block, with Tom Doniphon. Jimmy Stewart's Rans Stoddard represents the opposing characteristics that Doniphon proudly presents. He is not tough but is instead a smart, educated man of the future. He aims to bring learning and law to Shinbone. In

Horizons West, first published in 1969, Jim Kitses demonstrated the heart of the western as a conflict between civilization and wilderness (order and chaos). The binaries set up by Kitses illuminate the potential conflicts between the individual and the community, nature and culture, and the West and the East.[20] Responding to the popular auteur theory, Kitses argued that "while usefully offering a systematic approach in a period dominated by an elitist criticism of personal taste, auteurism presented problems."[21] Looking at films solely through the lens of authorship and the eye of the director ignored outside factors and preexisting tropes that were presented in the given genre. It is important to note that Kitses had set out to put auteurs into context, not to do away with them. In fact, the unique status of *The Man Who Shot Liberty Valance* is attributable not only to John Ford and his crew but to how the film operates within the entire genre. Without frontier legends interpreted on screen, the film would not have the purchase it continues to enjoy today.

Doniphon and Stoddard represent the opposition between order and chaos in the western in a shifting play that highlights "the genre's basic function, its enquiry into the roots and circumstances of American character."[22] In many ways, it was the settling of the Western frontier that finalized America's founding. *The Man Who Shot Liberty Valance* directly confronts the conflicts Kitses highlighted. The western is grounded in American identity; as Anne Butler has pointed out, its conventions help define who we are individually and as a nation. The genre raises questions about the Wild West: Was it an oasis threatened by the East? Or was it a savage land that needed to be settled? These are questions that have been taken on by numerous films throughout the western's long and successful tenure as one of the most popular genres in film history.

Historian Richard B. Ray has weighed in on how these oppositional binary conflicts are remedied in *The Man Who Shot Liberty Valance* by "showing the interpretation of the two sets of values, postures, and life-styles."[23] The East/West binary is represented by Ranse/Tom, law/gun, idealism/pragmatism, but also statehood/territory, conscience/pride, community/individual, and ultimately life/death. Of course, the film also treats female characters with a level of insensitivity, showing them as products of and not a participants in the foundation of modern civilization. This isn't the only shortcoming of *The Man Who Shot Liberty Valance,* however; as has been noted, the film is completely devoid of Native Americans.

Frontier scholar Richard Slotkin has argued that "in each stage of its development, the Myth of the Frontier relates the achievement of 'progress' to a particular form or scenario of violent action."[24] From Stoddard's robbery to Doniphon's killing of Liberty Valance (credited to Stoddard), the taming of the West in *The Man Who Shot Liberty Valance* was initiated and settled through violence. Interestingly, while discussing Hollywood and John Wayne in the 1960s, Slotkin completely overlooked *The Man Who Shot Liberty Valance* and instead focused on *The Alamo* (1960) to explore Wayne's stardom in the 50s and early 60s. Slotkin argued that a John F. Kennedy's heroic persona coupled with postwar growth and prosperity called for a modernization of Turner's frontier thesis. The good/evil binary, as made manifest in the US/USSR, capitalist/communist struggle offered a perfect opportunity to explore the conflict between wilderness and civilization on the American frontier. The United States was viewed as "exceptional" and to be "interpreted as proof of our vanguard or pioneer status among modern nations."[25]

Setting is a crucial element in Ford's westerns, many of which were filmed in the magnificent vista of Monument Valley, with is wide-ranging valleys and picturesque rock formations seemingly tailor made for cowboys to ride off in the sunset. However, *The Man Who Shot Liberty Valance* was not given the beautifully photographed Technicolor Monument Valley of *The Searchers* (1956). Instead, Ford filmed *The Man Who Shot Liberty Valance* primarily on the Paramount sound stages. The setting deglamorized the genre, making it look feeble and outdated. Famed historian Kevin Brownlow told me that the film's look always took him out of it, making it difficult to appreciate (he then explained this as a reason for me to write this book). The critique is understandable, especially once viewers get used to the Ford's other beautiful films.

Landscape in westerns is always an essential character. In *West of Everything*, Jane Tompkins posits that "it is the genius of the western that it seems to make the land speak for itself."[26] The terrain is often something to be endured, a test of sorts, that invokes a survival of the fittest. This is what makes *The Man Who Shot Liberty Valance* stand out. Ranse is not made for the frontier in its current form, but he seeks to survive by making the West a modern, law-abiding place for the future. Men like Tom Doniphon "imitate the land" as they "try to look as much like nature as possible."[27] The frontiersman often blends into his horse, who blends into the desert or mountains, creating a consistent mosaic that shows the character in his rightful place. Rans, on the other hand, works to bridge the frontier with a modern Eastern lifestyle. He looks out of place with his suit, bundle of books, and lofty ideas about a law-abiding future.

It is important to note that "the encounter of home and wilderness is more than a theme in Ford's westerns: It is a central, formative viewpoint, a way of looking at the world."[28] In Ford's 1939 *Stagecoach*, there is an early scene in a bar where we can see a horse looking in; there are also shots from within the stagecoach that show us the "savage" Indians

Figure 2. "Directed by John Ford" title card

riding up alongside, which allows us to see the frontier from inside the settled world. *The Searchers* has numerous shots from within the household that show us the wilderness through the front door. It is the same door through which Ethan (John Wayne) enters and leaves in the first and final shot of the film. The indoors and outdoors are in a constant juxtaposition that represents civilization and wilderness, order and chaos. The setting—frontier towns in the cavernous West—left Ford with a clean palette to create and recreate American ideals. As Kitses argued, Ford's "genius as a filmmaker was his unerring instinct for iconic designs and emblematic rituals, the horizon shots and words spoken over the grave that allowed him to humanize history and monumentalize the mundane."[29]

Almost every element of a Ford western is memorable and can be traced throughout his monumental career. The setting that emphasizes the standard conflict in the genre also brings the hero and villain to the forefront: "The typical Ford hero acted not for himself but for large causes—duty, honor, loyalty."[30] Of course, the loyalty and duty is what divides characters and creates the conflict. Those on the side of order will be fighting against the lawlessness that most settled communities strove for. The chaotic characters fight to keep the West unsettled and anarchic, so they remain free to reign as hell raisers without consequence.

As John Cawelti has noted, genres often move in a four-stage sequence—from a classic stage, which standardizes characters and story, to an "affirmation of myth" stage, where the classic genre comes back to connect with a new generation (*The Magnificent Seven, True Grit*), to a burlesque stage, which incorporates humor and critique (*Cat Ballou, Blazing Saddles*), and finally to demythologization (*Little Big Man, Soldier Blue*). *The Man Who Shot Liberty Valance*'s place in history was only further solidified by the films that came after. The death of the traditional hero and villain on the frontier gave way to a new lens through which to view the genre. With Ranse and Hallie making success of their progressive interests, they become the heroes of a new age. Bringing law and education to Shinbone ushered in opportunity for reflection. The genre continues to make good on that opportunity to this day, asking viewers to consider the trials and tribulations of progress.

3. | Women and the Western

Despite the genre's reputation of being a bit of a boy's club, influential female critics have weighed in on the western and even found a deep admiration for the genre and its interpretive potential. For example, while some historians have pointed to the stereotypical depictions of men, women, and Native Americans in John Ford's westerns, Gaylyn Studlar has argued that "Ford's Westerns present themselves as a mythic discourse on the epic forging of national identify."[1] It seems that those who understand the western as a canvas for exploring identity manage to make the best films and offer the most useful histories and, when necessary, criticisms. Before we get to Dorothy Johnson's short story that was the basis for Ford's film, it will be useful to examine a few female critics who have found a home on the range.

One of the most famous female voices to assess John Wayne and the western genre was Joan Didion, who spent time on the set of *The Sons of Katie Elder* (1965). Didion wrote that "when John Wayne rode through my childhood, and perhaps maybe yours, he determined forever the shape of certain of our dreams."[2] She understood the majestic quality that Wayne evoked, a characteristic that is possibly the most transcendent part of the genre. Didion remembers first seeing Wayne on screen and how he "suggested another world, one which may or may not have existed ever but in any case existed no more: a place where a man could move free, could make his own code and live by it; a world in which, if a man did what he had to do, he could one day take the girl and go riding through the draw and find himself home free."[3]

Despite the genre's prevailing reputation into the 1990s, Jane Tompkins confessed, "I make no secret of the fact: I love Westerns"[4] Tompkins continued, "Westerns satisfy a hunger to be in touch with something absolutely real."[5] The author noted that for much of the twentieth century, it was impossible to ignore westerns. Between the feature films, serials, and television shows, the western was a central part of American popular culture into the 1970s. Although much of the early canon was dominated by male characters, Tompkins noted that "stories about men (at least in our culture) function as stories about all people, women learn at an early age to identify with male heroes."[6] One reason, she argued, is that women have been "socialized to please others" and therefore "acquire early on the ability to sympathize with people whose circumstances are different from their own."[7] This ability to identify with others, one would hope, has become more universal since Tompkins' writing. Of course, Tompkins acknowledged our culture's historic interest in pushing male ideas as universal ideals. This power certainly has left female audiences longing for more, and Tompkins has argued that understanding how they work gives one some power over such narratives.

Tompkins also saw the western as "antilanguage," in that "doing, not talking, is what it values."[8] There is truth to this, of course, as the genre is full of lone, stoic heroes. Tomkins observed that the Westerner is not equipped with the education to elucidate his feelings. This is partially why Doniphon feels threatened by Ranse's inclusion of education in Shinbone. "The western hero's silence symbolizes a massive suppression of the inner life . . . men would rather die than talk."[9] This is precisely why as soon as Doniphon realizes that his time as the frontier leader is done, which includes the loss of his girl, he goes home and burns down his house. For such an externalized hero, acting out is much easier than internalizing an uncertain future. *The Man Who Shot Liberty Valance* depicts the formation of a social and cultural desire for a more evolved man. Ranse wanted the uneducated (including women and children) to learn the tools of a democracy instead of lording the land with machismo, as Doniphon had done.

Writing in 2017, Nancy Schoenberger argued that "the Western hero has remained an icon of masculinity, even if it belongs more to nostalgia than to current representations."[10] Indeed, the influx of female western heroes (and directors) who appeared in the years since her book's publication does not diminish the historical accuracy of the observation, nor does the fact that even in the genre's heyday, the male western hero was not without his critical flaws, especially in characters like Ethan Edwards in *The Searchers*. Schoenberger described *The Searchers* as "the apotheosis of John Ford and John Wayne's artistic collaboration, the most mature expression of the Western hero."[11] One may argue that without *The Searchers*, we wouldn't have had *The Man Who Shot Liberty Valance*. Wayne's Ethan Edwards showed vulnerability that opened the door for Doniphon's demise. The frontier hero was not to age well, especially in an era of continued cultural convergence. Ethan knew that his racism was not shared by all, a fact that provoked his return, alone, to the frontier. Tom Doniphon is similar in that he understands that he is needed if men like Liberty Valance are around. Once Valance is gone, Doniphon's time in the sun is over as well.

Legendary film critic Molly Haskell also has a history of appreciating not only westerns but John Wayne specifically. Wayne has been vilified for decades, just as has the genre he represents. There are many legends and lies surrounding Wayne, many stemming from a single (unfortunate) interview he gave to *Playboy* as he was sick and dying. Those who've studied the actor and the man know that his actions often defied the questionable rhetoric that he sometimes espoused. Haskell can always be counted on to champion classic Hollywood films, despite their decreasing popularity among the New York elite. Haskell considered Wayne "one of the great movie actors of all time," a take she fully knows is "not universally held among my fellow film critics and the folks back east."[12] She originally wrote the piece for the *Village Voice* in 1976 after visiting the set of *The Shootist*. After meeting Wayne, Haskell admitted that he was "larger than life in real life, too. It is not just a matter of size but of magnetism, of an authority that he wears as easily as his Western outfit."[13]

One of Haskell's observations exemplifies why Wayne was so perfect to play Tom Doniphon in *The Man Who Shot Liberty Valance*. His "right, reassuring voice evoke[s] four decades of movie roles, mingling, passing in review, eternally present in the here and now of memory."[14] Few screen legends, if any, carry with them the entirety of the roles they've played into every new film. Haskell was able to see through the shallow criticism of the actor to see that "Wayne represents to me those true conservative values—personal honor and integrity, individualism

Figure 3. Tom confronting Liberty Valance's men

with responsibility—that have long ago been abandoned by the party who pretends to honor them . . . it is Wayne who stands on all boarders, reconciling the warring ambiguities of which his political persona is a crude distortion."[15] The western genre and Wayne himself would not have been as popular as they were for so many decades if such popularity was grounded in jingoistic and racist politics. There was always something larger at stake, a fact sometimes missed by less insightful critics of the genre.

While there have been many stars of westerns, none is as monumental as Wayne, which makes him a perfect point at which to hinge discussions of the genre. In her essay, Haskell pointed out that it is incorrect to assert that Wayne "always plays John Wayne," because "he has played heroes who were fallible in different ways: sometimes wrongheaded, sometimes puritanical, sometimes ruthless, somethings drunken, sometimes shy, sometimes earthy, sometimes crotchety, but rarely mean-spirited and never petty."[16] Anyone who sees Wayne as an icon of some ideal of masculinity has either not seen his films or not watched them closely. The celebrated *Red River* (1948) has Wayne as a dictatorial cattle driver. Even his later films like *The Searchers* and *The Shootist* feature Wayne's character as quite far from any respectable masculine ideal. In the former, his Ethan Edwards is a racist yet loyal family man embodying deep and contradictory motives. In the latter, his J. B. Books works to instill his young fan (played by Ron Howard) that the gunfighters and frontiersman of the Wild West were nothing to make heroes out of. Haskell reminded readers that Wayne "makes no bones about wanting to play men with whom audiences can identify."[17]

Shoenberger admitted that Wayne and Ford admiration can feel something like a boy's club, but she found value in studying their constructed masculinity, as it reminded her of her own father. In what she jokingly referred to as her "John Wayne Problem," she related to the admiration in Joan Didion's essay "John Wayne: A Love Song." As a lifelong fan of Wayne-Ford westerns, she examined the larger implications of the collaboration. Schoenberger wrote, "At their best, the qualities and attributes that make men, at least in John Ford-John Wayne Westerns, are also qualities that define the finest of human behavior"[18] In other words, these films highlight what it means "to be peaceful but to be ready, to respect women, to be loyal to friends and family, to be willing and able to change your mind, to master yourself, to mentor the young, and to face the end with dignity."[19] These are all transcendent qualities of the western that speak to the enduring relevance and fascination with the frontier, myths and all.

MAKE WAY FOR DOROTHY JOHNSON

We can well imagine Dorothy M. Johnson bristling slightly at the assertion that westerns are for guys. Previous histories that detail John Ford's *The Man Who Shot Liberty Valance* offer little history or context on the story's author. Dorothy Johnson made a career out of writing stories that grappled with the primary characters of the American West. She had numerous stories made into Hollywood films with top directors and stars. The films include *The Hanging Tree* (1959), Gary Cooper's last film; *The Man Who Shot Liberty Valance* (1962), which landed the larger-than-life star power of John Wayne and Jimmy Stewart; and *A Man Called Horse* (1970), starring Richard Harris. In 2005, PBS aired a documentary on Johnson called *Gravel in her Gut and Pit in Her Eye.*

Johnson was born in McGregor, Iowa, on December 19, 1905, not the location one would assume for a writer who would become known for fictional stories about the American West. She died, however, in Missoula, Montana's Rattlesnake Valley. That sounds more like it. Upon her death in 1984, the seventy-eight-year-old writer was a highly decorated fiction veteran. Johnson won the Spur Award from the Wester Writers of America for her short story "Lost Sister." In 1976, she was given the Levi Strauss Golden Saddleman Award "for bringing dignity and honor to the history and legends of the West." Both John Wayne and John Ford would also be recipients of the same award.[20] Miss Johnson received numerous awards, including the Western Heritage Wrangler Award (1978), the Golden Saddleman Award (1976), an honorary doctorate from the University of Montana (1973), a University of Montana Distinguished Service Award (1961), and Montana's Outstanding Professional Woman of the Year (1952).

Johnson's family moved to Great Falls, Montana, in 1909 before moving on to Whitefish, Montana, in 1913. She grew up reading a great deal of history of the American West and along with it the fictional narratives that popularized the idea of the Wild West. While in Whitefish, Johnson got to know one of her father's friends, George Tayler, who was chief of police. Not only was Tayler the top cop in town, but he was also an old-time lawman, the kind who could be found "with his six-gun under his coat at church."[21] Johnson's biographer admits that legends of pioneers regaling the author with stories was largely invention born in dust-jacket blurbs, but we cannot discount the influence of Tayler and the model he provided as a frontier type that would manifest in her future works. Tayler also embodied frontiersman confidence with his knowledge of explosives, which he would use to take care of unwanted stumps in town. Johnson recalled that anyone "willing to use explosives to get rid of stumps was a public benefactor."[22] Of course, nobody knew where he got this expertise, something that perhaps added to his mythos.

When Johnson was young, the Whitefish City Hall "was a rattletrap frame building with a stable out back, built to shelter the official city horse."[23] Of course, by this time, there was no longer the need for a publicly accessible town horse. But such visuals set in motion a direct connection to the frontier days, just as anyone can imagine living in a world before they were born by recalling their surroundings from childhood. From Whitefish, Johnson enrolled at the University of Montana, where she studied under H. G. Merriam, the founder of *The Frontier* magazine, where some of her first stories would later appear. Wherever she found herself, Johnson interviewed old-timers for first-hand stories from the frontier days. After a rocky marriage, Johnson divorced her husband, paid off all the debt she was saddled with, and never married again. In fact, her tombstone reads "Paid."

Johnson moved from Washington State to Menasha, Wisconsin, for another stenographer position. She then moved to New York City for a job at Gregg Publishing. Johnson was in the city for fifteen years, during which time she deeply missed the American West. She wrote many stories of the West while situated in the concrete jungle of the Big Apple. The homesickness fueled great creativity. While in Manhattan, Johnson read any Wild West narrative she could from the New York Public Library. During this time, she also became editor for *The Woman* magazine, furthering her experience and status in the publishing industry.

Johnson recalled writing a story while she was in New York that relied on details about frontier-era six-shooters. She located a dealer and found an 1880 .44-caliber single-action Colt handgun. A police friend was frightened at the sight, knowing she needed a permit to even possess the weapon (as well as the several others she had acquired). Johnson eventually showed the curious law enforcement friends her vintage firearms. "I put them in a shopping bag with a bunch of carrots on top for camouflage," she wrote, "and trudged up the station house steps trying to look like an abused housewife, mother of seven, coming to report that her old man was on the sauce again and she didn't know which jail her oldest boy was in this time."[24] The cops were in awe of the classic guns as they "played Captain Kidd with the flintlock, Wild Bill Hickok with the Colt and Doc Holiday with the pepperbox."[25] She couldn't have found a better example of how the legends Wild West was still capturing hearts and minds.

Johnson returned to Whitefish in 1953, where she had graduated high school thirty-one years prior. Now working as editor of the *Whitefish Pilot,* she was living closer to the locations featured in her stories. Johnson also became secretary-manager of the Montana Press Association. During this time, she also taught in University of Montana's School of Journalism before retiring in 1967. Johnson wrote sixteen books and numerous short stories, many of which were anthologized in collections on the American West. Her home office was full of movie posters made from her stories, along with signed pictures from stars of those films. Johnson was quick to disclose how sweet Gary Cooper was. She reveled in communication with the stars, likely because there was always a mutual respect. People like Cooper and John Wayne, frequent western stars, certainly knew her work. Johnson was also known for featuring Native American characters, doing a great deal of research to make sure she represented their traditions accurately. As a result, Johnson was adopted into Blackfeet tribe and given the name Kills Both Places.

Few writers understood the application of the frontier mythos better than Dorothy Johnson. Her delight in the genre and her devotion to understanding the lived realities of frontier life inform her entire body of work. Johnson also singlehandedly dispelled the notion that westerns were written by and for men (or boys, of course). Her fascination with the frontier found common ground with the likes of Tompkins, Haskell, Shoenberger, and Didion. Yet it was Johnson among these luminaries whose interlocutors were real-life frontiersman at the ends of their days and whose own early life was formed within sight of the very frontier her works so richly explored.

"THE MAN WHO SHOT LIBERTY VALANCE"

One feature that made Johnson's work stand out is that her characters usually subverted the genre in some way. Understanding the frontier so deeply allowed her an informed creativity that lent useful criticism to the mythology around the Wild West. She read seemingly every story printed about the West. She knew the characters, locations, and narratives, and she learned how to bend the structure to make it her own. One thing that makes "The Man Who Shot Liberty Valance," both the story and film, so important is how Johnson sought to create a story that was different from the usual Wild West shootout climax. "The Man Who Shot Liberty Valance" was first published in *Cosmopolitan* in 1949 and then anthologized in 1953. To her dismay, the original story had an innocent error. At the end, Ranse and his wife rode off to an airport. The story ended in 1910, before commercial flight was commonplace. There weren't any airports to run off to! Before the story was published in *Indian Country*, Johnson was able to get a correction issued.

With the minor historical crisis averted in future printings, the story of Ranse Foster, Bert Barricune (Wayne's Tom Doniphon in the film), and Liberty Valance has at its heart everything the film does—a flashback from a funeral of an old Westerner, told by a man who was looking back at how he came to prominence. At the funeral was a young reporter, someone like Johnson herself, eager to hear stories of the old Wild West. The cactus rose was set atop the casket, just like in the film, signifying the feelings still present between Ranse's wife and Bert, her first love. Ranse told the reporter that Bert was a friend for decades, but the truth remained hidden: Bert "was my enemy, he was my conscience, he made me whatever I am."[26]

Figure 4. Ranse speaking with journalists, looking at his watch

A major difference is that in the film, we learn the truth when we see Tom (Bert) shoot Liberty Valance. In the story, it's clear from the start that Ranse is grappling with how he became who he was. "He was by no means ashamed of the man he finally became, except that he owed too much to other people." Ranse's psychology is examined throughout the story, whereas in the film, our understanding of Ranse builds toward the final scenes when we see him reflecting on his trajectory that made him who he was thanks to the assistance and sacrifice of many around him.

As in the film, Bert first finds Ranse, then a "tenderfoot," after Ranse's coach is robbed by Liberty Valance. The bruised and battered Ranse is left lying on the ground while Bert finds water and sets up camp. Bert has fun sizing up the Easterner, showing his dominance by gloating about his survivalist superiority, the kind of hypermasculine dalliance John Wayne perfected on the big screen. There was no question that Ranse was a fish out of water. Bert points to the closest town and rides off, forcing Ranse to walk for two days. For most of the story, Bert serves as a guardian to Ranse, whereas in the film, Wayne's Tom adds a reluctance to his support of Ranse. Tom knows his days of being the frontier hero are over, and Hallie leaves Tom for the new generation's hero, which culminates in Tom's meltdown as he set his house aflame.

When Ranse finally finds the marshal of Twotrees, it is clear that there are no enforceable laws in the region, although we learn that there is a bounty for anyone who apprehends Liberty Valance, who is guilty of some untold crime in the nearby law-abiding territory. Just as in the film, Ranse walks to a nearby café, where he meets Bert's girl, Hallie. Ranse is uncomfortable with how she pities him, giving him a meal after he offers to work for food. Looking back, Ranse realizes that the "tenderfoot" version of himself died on the prairie that day Valance decided to beat him unconscious for simply because he could.

Johnson's story has Ranse working multiple jobs, hitting rock bottom, as he serves meals at the café before stealing scraps from customers' plates after they leave. During this time, Ranse begins to practice shooting a Colt .45 he purchased from a drunkard. Whenever Bert sees Ranse, the situation turns into a confrontation. Bert revels in embarrassing Ranse. "A dog eats where it can," Bert observes condescendingly as Ranse eats scraps. When a job opens, Ranse takes work at a general store, working just enough to eat and buy cartridges for his gun. As in the film, locals realize Ranse is educated and able to teach reading and writing. Ranse begins the first school in Twotrees. Hallie is beyond excited to learn how to read, though she knows that Bert would not

Figure 5. Ransom Stoddard, Attorney at Law

think very highly of it. The tension between Hallie's interest in progress and Bert's dependence on the status quo is clear. Bert guilts Hallie over her desire to learn; still, she never misses a class.

Bert finds Ranse during a session of target practice. "I come out to tell you that Liberty Valance is in town. He's interested in the dude that anybody can kick around—this here tenderfoot that boasts how he can read Greek." Ranse rides into town, his gun clearly visible (something he hid until now). The town is strangely quiet, the street empty, the general store padlocked. Liberty Valance appears, walking down the street toward Ranse. The two approach each other. "I owe you something," said Ranse. Both men draw guns and fire. Valance is killed, and Ranse takes a round in the shoulder. Bert tells Ranse that Ranse's shot missed, so Bert fires as well. "I don't generally miss," Bert said.

Figure 6. Hallie helping Ranse

The only reason Bert let people believe Ranse killed Liberty Valance is because he could see that the future was with people like Ranse. Hallie fell for Ranse, and Bert loved Hallie, so what was good for her was good for him. A Westerner, aged fifty, was a senior citizen in 1910. As Johnson wrote, Bert became "an unwanted relic of the frontier that was gone, a legacy to more civilized times that had no place for him." Johnson's story ends with Ranse reminding Hallie that Bert always wanted the best for her. He was willing to give up his place in her life for her to live in the future that was inevitable, a future that no longer needed men like him.

Ford wanted to put this story in a larger context, beyond that of just a personal reflection. As Joseph McBride and Michael Wilmington pointed out, in Johnson's story, "Stoddard mulls over the events as he returns to town for a funeral, but he does not reveal the truth to anyone. Ford changed things so that Stoddard would confess the truth to society's watchdogs, the newspapermen."[27] The authors also suggested that Ford may have been channeling a 1955 television movie he directed called *Rookie of the Year,* in which a sportswriter, Mike Cronin, (played by John Wayne), refuses to print the real story of disgraced baseball legend Buck Garrison (Ward Bond), a clear nod to Shoeless Joe Jackson, who was part of the 1919 Black Sox scandal. Garrison had changed his name to Goodhue and kept his role in the 1919 fixed World Series a secret from his son, Lyn. Garrison's son, played by Patrick Wayne, is a rising baseball star, and Cronin decides not to print his historical column to save the kid any negativity his father's past might have on Lyn's own career.

Johnson sold the rights to John Ford for $7,500 in March of 1961. Ford biographer Joseph McBride has noted that the director's interest in this story had as much to do with Ford's passion for the American West as with his interest in mysteries. Ford's films always operate on a wavelength that both engages history and becomes a piece of its own narrative world. As McBride tells is, "Ford used filmmaking as his refuge from reality, a way to create a safe, privileged, mythical world that functioned according to his own private rules" and always accompanied by his "large extended family of actors and crew people."[28]

Ford's career had spanned the entirety of feature filmmaking. Peter Bogdanovich penned an appreciation of Ford in 1967 and filmed a documentary titled *Directed by John Ford* (1971), which is the primary audiovisual evidence of Ford's sometimes grumpy demeanor. For example, when Bogdanovich asked Ford how he shot the land-rush scene in *3 Bad Men* (1926), Ford responded curtly, "with a camera." Bogdanovich

Figure 7. Hallie and Link catching up

was visiting the set of *Cheyanne Autumn* (1964), Ford's latest feature western, as part of a writing assignment from *Esquire* magazine. Bogdanovich had interviewed many people associated with Ford and heard all the legends, most of which Ford associates maintained were true, including the time a studio sent Ford a man saying the film was two days behind schedule. He was shooting about five pages per day, so Ford "leafed through [the script], counted out ten pages, ripped them out, tossed them in the air, and told the man to tell his boss they were now back on schedule. And he never did shoot those ten pages."[29] Legends aside, Ford was the perfect director for Johnson's story. His career with the genre spanned the history of cinema itself, from the early silent days to the present. Who better to visualize the transition of the American West from wilderness to civilization?

Dorothy Johnson had many interesting engagements with Hollywood throughout her career. Besides having her stories adapted into films, she was once asked to ghostwrite the autobiography of "America's Sweetheart" Mary Pickford, the wildly popular actress and entertainer who cofounded United Artists in 1919. For a lunch with Pickford to discuss the project, Johnson purchased a new dress for the occasion, since she was unused to sharing a table with such royalty. Johnson whimsically recalled going to Pickford's swanky apartment:

> I went over to this $1,500 [per month] apartment and got myself past the doorman and past the elevator man and past another man whom I never did figure out. Up at Miss Pickford's door I came to the butler. I handed him my coat because the only other butler I had ever met in my life had done nothing but yearn to put my coat somewhere. I don't know what Miss Pickford's butler did because he looked as though he had never had a coat in his hands before in his life.[30]

The conversation with the legendary actress went well. Pickford spoke candidly about many events she didn't want covered in the book (and all things Johnson would want to write). Ultimately, Pickford got someone else to write the book. Johnson assumed she was too gentle on Pickford, "I couldn't scare her into doing anything!"[31]

Johnson explained that her writing always began with an emotion she hoped to explore. Most common, she felt, were pity and admiration. Her ideas came from a wide range of personal experiences traveling the West, from reading western fiction and history, and from Hollywood films and television shows. Johnson enjoyed seeing the oft-used trope of a hero slowly and confidently walking down the street looking to take down the villain. "It was new, I suppose, when Owen Wister used it in *The Virginian*," Johnson wrote. "It had wonderful suspense. But it's worn out now—and the reason it got worn out is that it was good."[32] However, Johnson knew when to turn the tables on a predictable situation. This is what makes "The Man Who Shot Liberty Valance" so important. The story lures us with the promise of a shootout but gives us a conclusion that defies the expectations drawn from years of Hollywood shootouts. Admirers of Johnson's work appreciate how the author refused to force twentieth-century values into nineteenth-century settings. She also refused to lean into common stereotypes of western characters, including Native Americans.

The western genre has been much maligned in recent decades, often by people who know little of its history. Many disparage the western as inherently racist without knowing how truly subversive the genre was throughout its history. Such critics have clearly failed to account for such classics as *Johnny Guitar* (1954), *Forty Guns* (1957), *Little Big Man* (1970), and *Unforgiven* (1992), to say nothing of the work of Dorothy Johnson. The genre has also attained a prestige status in recent decades, though television westerns have grown in popularity most recently with the smash hit *Yellowstone* and its spinoffs within the Taylor Sheridan universe. Western-adjacent shows like *Justified* have also kept the genre in the public consciousness. Art films such as Jane Campion's *The Power of the Dog* (2021) have also found a home on the range. When outspoken actor Sam Elliott slammed the film for not adequately representing the West, Campion clapped back by calling Elliott a "bitch" and saying, "There's a lot of room on the range."[33] She followed by quipping more lightheartedly, "Ok, Sam, let's meet down at the Warner Bros. lot for a shootout!"[34]

Author Don Coldsmith recalled the moment during his first Western Writers of America convention (Coldsmith would later become president of the organization) when a small, doddering Dorothy Johnson walked in. Coldsmith turned to a fellow writer, Nelson Nye, in awe of how the woman's small stature did not align with her grand, often violent work. Coldsmith remembered thinking that "she looks like somebody's grandma, and she writes such violent stuff." Nye said, "Well, yeah, when Dorothy shoots somebody you know that son of a bitch is shot don't you?"[35] Johnson was known for using violence to make a point, never to celebrate such action. In this sense, her stories subvert the mythos of the Wild West that sells an image of gunslingers and outlaws running wild from town to town and train robbery to train robbery.

4. | Adapting the Legend

The screenplay for *The Man Who Shot Liberty Valance* was submitted by James Warner Bellah and Willis Goldbeck on March 20, 1961. The two were given twelve weeks to complete the script, with an additional four weeks for revisions following producer feedback. Bellah and Goldbeck were each paid $30,000 for the screenplay—$10,000 upon signing the contract, another ten grand for finishing the script, and the final ten for submitting revisions. Ford would receive $150,000 to direct and produce the picture, paid in four installments.

Represented by MCA, James Stewart signed his contract with John Ford Productions on April 5. The actor signed for $300,000 ($25,000 per week for twelve weeks) plus 10 percent of the gross receipts, which would be adjusted down should another major star get involved (which was expected). Stewart was to receive top billing with Wayne, along with approval of costars and their billing positions. Should Ford drop out, Stewart was also given approval of the replacement director. He also retained approval of script if Ford was for any reason unable to supervise the screenwriters. Stewart trusted Ford completely, only showing equivocation if Ford was not involved. Stewart had just finished filming *Two Rode Together* and certainly acquired a deep respect and admiration for the man. "I love him," Stewart said years later in conversation with Bogdanovich. "He's just . . . he's a genius."[1] Stewart was especially impressed with how Ford could translate a script into moving visuals.

Wayne singed his contract the day after Stewart. Ford naturally wanted his longtime star and collaborator for the film. The Duke was a primary piece of the Ford Stock Company, a continually used combination of cast and crew who all knew how to work with each other. They had an artistic shorthand, trusted each other, and were always willing to avoid lengthy skirmished by hashing them out quickly (often with fists). Wayne was to be paid $750,000 for the film, with an additional 7.5 percent gross (Stewart's take of the gross was then dropped to match Wayne's). If production exceeded twelve weeks, Wayne would be paid $25,000 per week, the same as Stewart. Top billing was up for debate. Stewart agreed to a coin toss—another sign of mutual respect between the two legendary stars. Stewart must have lost the toss, as the first title card went to Wayne, followed by Stewart.

The Duke was in a long-term contract with Paramount, so Ford brokered a deal with his own production company to coproduce *The Man Who Shot Liberty Valance*. The budget was $3,207,000, half of which was raised by Ford. The picture had 75 percent ownership by Paramount, with 25 percent for John Ford Productions. The contract allowed for twelve years for distribution to recoup the investment. If the film made its investment back, Paramount would keep distribution rights for another six months. Paramount allowed for a maximum production overrun of 30 percent and a maximum number of feet filmed at 9,500. Production was scheduled to begin on September 5, 1961, at Paramount Studios. No Monument Valley was needed for this picture. Ford was given five months to complete any reshoots and editing prior to general release. Ford also asked to have his son Pat on as a production assistant for $25,000. Paramount agreed to $7,500.

The film reached immortal status thanks to the Hollywood addition of the famous line about printing the legend, which speaks to this and almost every other western. When *The Man Who Shot Liberty Valance* was completed, Johnson was amused at how the character names were changed; Bert Barricune became Tom Doniphon and Ransome Foster became Ransome Stoddard. John Wayne sent her an autographed photo with an inscription that quipped, "Have you anyone else you want shot?" Liberty Valance remained, however, though after seeing Lee Marvin's performance, she said, "I never dreamed up such a dastardly villain."[2]

Because the original story was short, the film adaptation had to expand the narrative. It needed new characters and a more detailed location. The film noted the "picketwire," denoting the Purgatoire River in Colorado. Johnson's story never specified a location, but she did envision Ranse practicing with his pistol on the Cheyenne Reservation in Montana.

Following the film's release, James Warner Bellah signed a contract to publish a novelization of the movie. Johnson found it odd that she would get paid to have her story adapted into a movie, and then the movie could get adapted back into a book. Because Johnson had a good agent, she was able to get paid for the novelization as well; her fee for the rights was $1,000. The dean at the university quipped, "Dorothy, I always knew what you are. Now I know what your price is."[3] Steve Smith's biography of Johnson, titled *The Years and the Wind and the Rain*, offers minimal insight into "The Man Who Shot Liberty Valance." Perhaps this is because it was a short story, and the film came out near the end of her career. The movie certainly gained more respect with time, much of that following her death in 1984. One can wonder if she

Figure 8. Liberty Valance holding newspaper with headline "Liberty Valance Defeated"

realized how important her story was, though the cast and crew of the film adaptation certainly treated her with warmth. The great symbol and heart of Johnson's story, the cactus rose, was given significant placement in the film.

Bellah and Goldbeck's script was sent off for Production Code approval. In 1961, the Production Code Administration was then just a shell of its former self as an industry censorship office. PCA head Geoffrey Shurlock advised Paramount Pictures that the scene where Ransom gets kicked "is unacceptably brutal and should be eliminated." The same went for other scenes, including "the beating of Peabody."[4] Other mentions of prostitutes were to be excised, but for the most part, any objections on the part of the censors were minor. Of course, by the 1960s, filmmakers were getting away with controversial content on a level previously unknown to a Hollywood director. Of course, John Ford was a man of the old guard and was already a master at making films within the Production Code guidelines that had been present for most of his career.

No filmmaker had a résumé that reflected the American frontier like John Ford's, whose corpus of works dated from 1917's *Straight Shooting*, starring Harry Carey, and wound its way through *The Iron Horse* (the monumental railroad epic that appeared in1924), *Stagecoach* (which made John Wayne a star in 1939), *My Darling Clementine* (which in 1946 featured Henry Fonda as Wyatt Earp), *The Searchers* (1956), and *Two Rode Together* (another Jimmy Stewart vehicle that in 1961 was the film just prior to *The Man Who Shot Liberty Valance*). Having survived Hollywood through numerous industry changes (silent to sound, black-and-white to color film, transition to widescreen), Ford continued to work at the peak of his powers for arguably longer than any other filmmaker. Ford, like many others, hired the same talent throughout the years, preferring to work with actors he knew and trusted.

Central to bringing *The Man Who Shot Liberty Valance* to life was the western pedigrees of the film's talented crew. Cinematographer William H. Clotheir served as the director of photography for several westerns, including John Wayne's *The Alamo* (1960), John Ford's *The Horse Soldiers* (1959), and Budd Boetticher's *7 Men from Now* (1956). Legendary costume designer Edith Head, perhaps best known for her work with Alfred Hitchcock, also had a track record with westerns. One of her first costume jobs in Hollywood was on Victor Fleming's *The Virginian* (1929), starring a young Gary Cooper. Through the years, she contributed to numerous B westerns and eventually graduated to films like *The Furies* (1950), *Shane* (1953), *Gunfight at the O.K. Corral* (1957), and *Last Train from Gun Hill* (1959). Having worked on a range of westerns with various directors, showing that they understood the look and feel of the genre, both Clotheir and Head were both primed to help Ford transfer his elegiac vision of the West to the big screen.

The supporting cast of *The Man Who Shot Liberty Valance* offers a cross section of film and TV westerns dating back decades. John Carradine created a memorable role as the dubious Hatfield in *Stagecoach* (1939), in addition to roles in several other 1930s westerns, including John Ford's *Drums along the Mohawk* (1939). Carradine also had roles in the anti-McCarthy *Johnny Guitar* (1954) and roles in several TV westerns. Before getting noticed in Sergio Leone's *The Man with No Name* trilogy opposite Clint Eastwood, Lee Van Cleef began his career in the iconic *High Noon* (1952). He would star in many respectable crime films before appearing in TV westerns such as *Annie Oakley* and *Wagon Train*. Andy Devine, a ubiquitous, gravel-voiced presence in films and on TV from the 1950s on, also had a role in Ford's *Stagecoach*, as well as parts in lesser-known westerns such as *Frisco Sal* (1945) and *The Last Bandit* (1949), before being cast in Ford's *Two Rode Together*.

Edmond O'Brien is best known for his turns as noir protagonists in films like *The Killers* (1946), *D.O.A.* (1949), and *711 Ocean Drive* (1950), giving him less experience in westerns than many of his costars, but his recent stints in *Laramie* and *Zane Grey Theatre* showed that his tough-guy persona translated well into the frontier narrative. O'Brien worked in theater before beginning film work in 1939. After serving in World War II. he landed several roles in noir films and eventually won a Best Supporting Actor Oscar for his work in *The Barefoot Contessa* (1954).

Football star turned Hollywood actor Woody Strode was a staple of John Ford's late-career westerns. While playing football at UCLA, Strode, along with Ray Bartlett, Kenny Washington, and Jackie Robinson, were part of an undefeated 1939 Bruins team. Robinson, of course, went on

Figure 9. Wayne and O'Brien at the table

to break the color barrier in Major League Baseball. After a stint in the US Army Air Corps during World War II, Strode played pro football for the Los Angeles Rams, becoming, along with Kenny Washington, the first two Black athletes to play in the NFL. Though he had been dabbling in film appearances since 1941, acting became a regular gig by the 1950s. Strode found rising stardom after being cast in *Spartacus* (1960).

Strode went on to play important roles in Ford's *Sergeant Rutledge* (1960) and *Two Rode Together* (1961) and would go on to play memorable roles in other westerns such as *The Professionals* (1966) and *Once Upon a Time in the West* (1968). Strode came to work with Ford late in the director's life. In his memoir, Strode described Ford as "a romantic and a dreamer. He was an artist, although he would never admit it."[5] Many fans of Ford today equate the filmmaker with his cantankerous late-life interviews. While Strode did see the grouchy-old-man version of John Ford, he nonetheless kept coming back to work with him over the years. "Ford liked to see himself as one of the troops rather than the chief," wrote Strode, "and when he made a friendship, it was lasting."[6] Ford quickly won Strode's respect when he fought to cast him over Sidney Poitier or Harry Belafonte, two established Black stars, in *Sergeant Rutledge*. Warner Bros. wanted the established stars, but Ford didn't believe that they could act tough enough. Ford went to bat and won. He then sent Strode to an Arizona ranch to learn how to ride horses and move like a cavalryman. The training paid off as the director cast Strode in three more of his films.

Perhaps best known for her work in Alfred Hitchcock's *Psycho* (1960), Vera Miles also had a history with Ford. She played the educated frontier woman Laurie Jorgensen in *The Searchers* (1956), a character that was in many ways opposite the one she would play in *The Man Who Shot Liberty Valance*. Adding to her western resume, Miles starred in Jacques Tourneur's *Wichita* (1955) as well as episodes of *Rawhide* and *Laramie*. Miles's additional work for Hitchcock included *The Wrong Man* (1956), with Henry Fonda, as well as the pilot episode of *Alfred Hitchcock Presents*. Miles was always a reliable character actor with the star quality of a leading woman. Few actors could hold their ground between larger-than-life figures like Stewart and Wayne, but Miles was one who could. Miles, still alive as of this writing, has not written a memoir and has been out of public view for many years. There is little written about her, sadly. Hopefully, someone will come across (or get access to) Miles's papers to write a history that will give her the due she has earned in the pantheon of Hollywood talent.

Lee Marvin, one of the great tough guys in midcentury Hollywood cinema, began his career with B westerns like *Hangman's Knot* (1952) but also landed a role in Raoul Walsh's *Gun Fury* (1953), starring Rock Hudson and Donna Reed, and Budd Boetticher's *7 Men from Now* (1956). Known primarily for sadistic villains in *The Big Heat* (1953), *Bad Day at Black Rock* (1955), *Violent Saturday* (1955), he was perfect for the title antagonist in *The Man Who Shot Liberty Valance*. Another stand-out role is Marvin's villain Bill Masters in *7 Men from Now* (1956), directed by Budd Boetticher. The film's final scene is legendary, and Marvin's Masters is memorably flummoxed after Randolph Scott's sheriff draws and shoots before Masters can think to draw his own revolvers.

Marvin later went on to play memorable tough-guy roles in *The Killers* (1964), *The Dirty Dozen* (1967), and *The Big Red One* (1980). Marvin was a life-long admirer of John Ford, and the director was drawn to Marvin for the role of Liberty Valance after seeing Marvin with John Wayne in *The Comancheros* (1961). No one could have been better for the role of Valance, as Marvin portrayed a character so detestable that even Dorothy Johnson was taken aback.

John Wayne and Jimmy Stewart took two completely different trajectories in the western, making their pairing so perfect for *The Man Who Shot Liberty Valance*. Wayne always played the dominant Westerner, the toughest guy in town, defender of justice, the textbook image of rugged individualism in everything from B films like *Ride Him, Cowboy* (1932) and *The Telegraph Trail* (1933) to *Stagecoach*, *Red River* (1948), *Rio Bravo* (1959), and beyond. One could critique Wayne for playing the same character in nearly every film, but that should not be seen as a problem if it works so well. His entire career can be seen as an investigation into masculinity, moving from hypermasculine frontier heroes to conflicted protagonists, culminating in *The Shootist* (1976), where the cancer-stricken gunfighter contemplates the purpose of his violent

Figure 10. Liberty Valance standing over Ranse

past. Wayne was not just well cast for many of Ford's westerns; he was essential for *The Man Who Shot Liberty Valance.* Wayne's biographer, Scott Eyman, observed that Wayne's character Ethan Edwards in *The Searchers* was pushed "towards a final ascendance to myth," while in *The Man Who Shot Liberty Valance,* Ford "begins with myth and methodically dismantles it on the way to a mournful irony, utterly undercutting the newspaperman's aphorism" (when the legend becomes fact, print the legend).[7] Ford used Wayne to brilliantly build and deconstruct myth. There was no other actor who could have been the Doniphon cornerstone of this film.

Conversely, Stewart regularly portrayed characters who were defined by traits other than hypermasculinity. His characters were often vulnerable, most famously in Frank Capra's *It's a Wonderful Life* (1946), but readily apparent in many westerns, ranging from the oddly comic *Destry Rides Again* (1939) and the string of Anthony Mann westerns *Winchester '73* (1950), *The Naked Spur* (1953), *The Far Country* (1954), and *The Man from Laramie* (1955). Stewart eventually worked with Ford in *Two Rode Together*, playing opposite often intimidating leading man Richard Widmark. Ford knew that Stewart was the exemplary persona to highlight the evolving Westerner, opposite John Wayne. In the years leading up to *The Man Who Shot Liberty Valance*, Stewart had played a wider range of conflicted characters, such as the obsessive protagonists in Hitchcock's *Rear Window* (1954) and *Vertigo* (1958). In an interview with Peter Bogdanovich, Stewart reflected beautifully on the real meaning of movies, defining them as "pieces of time."[8] That's exactly what *The Man Who Shot Liberty Valance* has become, both a piece of time, capturing a moment of Ford's reflection, a changing genre, but also something that would become timeless in its own way.

John Ford's *The Man Who Shot Liberty Valance* began production in September 1961. Ford's most emphatically supportive biographer, Joseph McBride, has argued that the film is the director's "artistic summation," and while Ford may have been "behind his time in most superficial ways, he was ahead of the public consciousness in more important aspects."[9] The film's timelessness, rooted in its ability to question the genre's mythology, is second to none. The film's power, to be sure, builds from Johnson's ability to shift genre expectations, questioning the nature of heroism and the stories told about heroes.

5. | No Stunning Vistas Here

"Hollywood, it's over," John Ford quipped in an interview three years after the release of *The Man Who Shot Liberty Valance*.[1] The director knew he was nearing the end of his career when he was shooting *The Man Who Shot Liberty Valance*. Ford also understood that the Hollywood he knew was disappearing fast. "In the United States they only have eyes for television," Ford continued.[2] The director's elegiac western can be seen as not only his last masterpiece but also the final word on the death of the frontier during the genre's classical period. *The Man Who Shot Liberty Valance* shot for forty-three days, from September 5 to November 9, 1961. It was only five days behind schedule, with a total production cost of $3,294,000, including $87,000 over the contracted budget. In the middle of filming, Paramount vice president George Weltner argued that "our market has reached the highest selectivity since the inception of the industry" because "the standard of demand has skyrocketed."[3] Weltner noted *The Man Who Shot Liberty Valance* specifically, as well as the internationalization of audiences, something that would help the Ford production as John Wayne continued to hold a large global fan base throughout the 1960s. The summer before production began, Paramount president Barney Balaban also cited *The Man*

Who Shot Liberty Valance as one of the "better quality pictures" yet to come from the studio's current slate.[4]

Most of the film was shot on stages at Paramount Studios. Exteriors like the train station and Tom Doniphon's house were filmed outside on the MGM backlot. Many wondered why John Ford, known for beautiful, expansive location shoots, would set this western primarily in town with cheap-looking sets. In fact, when I told legendary film historian Kevin Brownlow that I was writing this book, he hit me with the same questions. Why does this film look like a TV western? Perhaps that distracted him from the bigger picture Ford was getting at. Ford biographer Tag Gallagher posited that *The Man Who Shot Liberty Valance* "focuses on the town, as opposed to the range; statehood as opposed to territory, civilization as opposed to wilderness; words (law and education) as opposed to the gun . . . the past as prelude."[5] Ford was notorious for not giving straight answers to questions regarding his artistry. Fortunately, the answers are all on the screen. The end of the frontier is a not a celebration of the open range. Instead, the victory is for progress, the death of the Wild West bullies who stood in the way of the future.

Ford himself has spoken about his love of filming on the open rage. "My favorite location is Monument Valley, which lies where Utah and Arizona merge," said Ford. "It has rivers, mountains, plains, desert, everything the land can offer. I feel at peace there. I have been all over the world, but I consider this the most complete, beautiful place on earth."[6] So much of Ford's résumé leans on the beauty of Monument Valley. The lack of lavish landscape in *The Man Who Shot Liberty Valance* should not be seen as a shortfall but rather a deliberate choice made to help highlight the film's essential commentary on the stories we tell about the closing of the frontier.

Ford biographer Scott Eyman also noted the film's purposefully bland aesthetic, where "the landscape is almost completely absent, and Ford's eye for composition is muted . . . but the thematic resonance more than compensates for the fact that it's an old man's movie."[7] Ford was looking back at a career, at a life, and at the history he had spent decades depicting on screen. Paramount likely wanted Ford to shoot in color because it would be an easier sale to license for television, which was increasingly telecast in color. However, this melancholic tale about a man confronting his past, realizing his success was based on a lie, translates best in black and white. Not to mention the aged makeup of the characters, which would appear fake and forced in color. Think about how well the aging makeup comes across in *Citizen Kane* (1941), and now picture how it would look in color. Case closed.

There was no question that Ford was getting old and that *The Man Who Shot Liberty Valance* was likely to be the master's last great effort (even though he would make other films in the coming years). As a very old man at sixty-seven, Ford's eyesight was going in the one good eye he had left. In Dan Ford's biography of his grandfather, he recalled speaking to cast members who all spoke of the director's "lack of energy" on the set.[8] The film is an old man's tale, to be sure, and who better to direct than a man feeling his age? During filming, Wayne accepted an award at the Beverly Hilton. When Ford rose to introduce Wayne, he stumbled on the stairs. John Wayne, as usual, was right there near Papa Ford. Eyman writes that "Wayne, sensitive to the older man's wounded vanity, got up and made the same stumble, sliding down two stairs until he righted himself. The audience, thinking it was part of a joke, roared, but Wayne had successfully covered up his idol's deteriorating eyesight."[9]

Most of the scenes in *The Man Who Shot Liberty Valance* were shot on Paramount's Stage 9. One of the older stages, built in 1918, Stage 9 is also connected to Stage 8, has one side covered with offices, part of which is home to the studio's art department. Connected as well was the studio's schoolhouse, where child actors where tutored "rather haphazardly between takes on the soundstages."[10] Billy Wilder filmed scenes for *Double Indemnity* (1944) on Stage 9, and Hitchcock had the entire *Rear Window* (1954) set constructed here. Stage 9 was home to *Sunset Boulevard* and there, scenes were shot for *When Worlds Collide* (1951), *Gunfight at the O.K. Corral* (1957), *Breakfast at Tiffany's* (1961), *Seven Days in May* (1964), *Rosemary's Baby* (1968), and several *Star Trek* shows and films. For *The Man Who Shot Liberty Valance*, Stage 9 was used for Swede's kitchen, the dining room, main street in Shinbone, the *Shinbone Star* office, and Hank's saloon.

John Wayne grew increasingly frustrated with how Ford directed scenes in a manner that gave pivotal movements to other actors. Wayne's beef wasn't just with John Ford: Wayne complained that Howard Hawks did the same thing. Wayne got his confidence back when the filmed the scene where Liberty Valance knocks the steak out of Ransom's hands. Wayne comes in and starts an altercation with Valance, kicking the steak away from another customer who tries to pick it up. Ford was contemplating cutting the scene short, with Doniphon pushing Ranse back into the kitchen. Ford asked Stewart what he thought, and fortunately for Wayne, Stewart thought the scene was stronger with Wayne stepping up to Valance (complete with kicked steak).

This was a difficult film for Wayne, on many levels, because so much of the story both revolved around him and focused elsewhere. Speaking with Peter Bogdanovich, Duke explained the characters, commending

Figure 11. Hallie helping Ranse while Tom and Pompey stand nearby

Lee Marvin ("flamboyant heavy"), Edward O'Brien ("Intellectual humor"), Andy Devine and Jimmy Stewart ("kicking the horseshit"), and Vera Miles, who falls for the other guy. "So what the hell?" Wayne lamented. "Where do I go?"[11] Wayne assured Bogdanovich that he was never unhappy while filming *The Man Who Shot Liberty Valance*. Perhaps Wayne was just realizing that Ford's tale of the passing of the frontier was, on another level, also about the waning of Wayne's star image.

Stage 18 was another often used location for *The Man Who Shot Liberty Valance*. First used as a carpentry shop, Stage 18 was known as the DeMille Stage because he shot many of his early epics there before the stage was built in 1941. This was also the stage where Billy Wilder's *Sunset Boulevard* and DeMille's *Samson and Delilah* (1949) were shot. Stage 18 was also home to *Bonanza* (1959–73), scenes from *The Graduate*

Figure 12. Liberty, Ranse, and Tom standing in the dining room

(1967), *Black Rain* (1989), Jack Ryan's house in *Patriot Games* (1992), and the *Rear Window*–inspired *Disturbia* (2007).

Paramount's Stage 4 housed the interior of the school room (where Ranse educated the community), the convention hall (*Hollywood Reporter* noted that Ford asked for 150 extras for the convention scene), the old Drury lobby, and Handy's office, where Ranse learns that Tom shot Liberty Valance and where Ranse accepts his nomination.[12] Originally built in 1918, Stage 4 was utilized for scenes in *I Married a Witch* (1942), *The Blue Dahlia* (1946), *Union Station* (1950), *The Man Who Knew Too Much*, *El Dorado* (1966), and *The Last Tycoon* (1975).

The Valance gang's stagecoach holdup was the first scene shot for the film, on Paramount's Stage 5. As most of the stages at Paramount, 5 has a storied history and was used for Norma Desmond's house in

Sunset Boulevard. (1950), numerous sets for *Shane* (1953), police station and Ambrose Chapel in *The Man Who Knew Too Much* (1956), numerous interiors for *Vertigo* (1958), sets for *The Brady Bunch* (1969–74) and the Oval Office set in *Veep* (2012–15). Stage 5 was also used for large blood drives during World War II. The stage also had one wall dressed for westerns, making it a logical location for *The Man Who Shot Liberty Valance.*

Lee Marvin was nervous about beginning shooting because his nose had recently been broken while filming an episode of *Route 66* (1960–64), directed by Sam Peckinpah, when during a fight scene, Martin Milner accidentally connected on a fake punch. Marvin's face became swollen, and the actor was sure John Ford would replace him as Liberty Valance. The real reason the stagecoach robbery was filmed first was because Marvin would appear with a bandana covering his swollen nose. Marvin reveled in his role as Liberty Valance, even naming one of his dogs Liberty. Marvin's biographer, Dwayne Epstein, perfectly summarized Valance as someone who "conveyed the anger, maliciousness, and sadism of a man who symbolized all the lawlessness of the old west, and who refused to step gently aside to encroaching civilization."[13] Marvin's Valance was perhaps the meanest villain in the entire western genre. Marvin's Valance, with Ford's approval, expressed true brutality on the set, such as when he shoves an entire newspaper sheet into Peabody's mouth. He really had to shove that paper down Edmond O'Brien's throat, which makes the character that much more terrorizing. It was "fun for me to play that dangerously," recalled Marvin, "and get paid for it, too, and not kill anybody!"[14] Marvin's Liberty Valance put the actor on the map as a primary heavy for the coming decades.

Everyone wanted to work with Ford, including Marvin. But often the cast and crew found themselves the targets of the director's wrath.

John Wayne was often the victim of Ford's most vicious attacks. Lee Van Cleef remembered that Ford "was a complete bastard to Wayne."[15] Ford's biographer Joseph McBride wrote of a time when Wayne suggested something to Ford on set. "Jesus Christ," said an enraged Ford. "I take you out of eight-day Westerns, I put you in big movies, and you give me a stupid suggestion like that?"[16] Some have implied that Ford was increasingly tough on Wayne over the years for not serving in World War II. On set, Ford (Navy), Stewart (Army/Air Force), O'Brien (Army/Air Force), and Marvin (Marines) had all served, while Duke remained safely the celluloid hero.

Many members of the cast recalled similar stories, always remembering that Wayne got it worst of all. Marvin enjoyed the bullying, seeing it more as sport. Ford "was a bright motherfucker to screw around with, and I used to have fun teasin' him."[17] Perhaps Ford knew he met his match when the two first met on set. "Well, chief," said Marvin, "when the admiral comes aboard, the first mate has to pipe him in."[18] Marvin maintained that the two never had an issue. Jimmy Stewart, for some reason, was let off the hook consistently. Nobody understood why. But Stewart's golden child status didn't last forever.

One of the last scenes shot was the Doniphon funeral. During the set-up for the small funeral scene, Ford asked Stewart what he thought of Strode's costume. The actor was made up to look older, of course, including overalls and a hat. Stewart, telling the story to Peter Bogdanovich, responded to Ford by saying, "Waall, s'a little Uncle Remus, isn't it?"[19] Stewart was referring to a character with long history in African American folktales and popularized by James Baskett's character in the now blacklisted Disney film *Song of the South* (1946). "And what's wrong with Uncle Remus?" asked the director, as Stewart wished he had simply complimented the wardrobe. Ford was miffed because he put the costume together himself and was quite proud of it. The director then called in the rest of the cast and crew to see Strode's costume. "Looks like Uncle Remus, doesn't it?" Everyone chimed in affirmatively and affectionately, "like a bunch of parrots," added Stewart. Ford wasn't done, however. "One of the players seems to have some objection! One of the players here doesn't seem to like Uncle Remus! As a matter of fact, I'm not at all sure he even likes negroes!" Stewart nearly made it through the whole production without landing on the business end of one of Ford's grievances. Meanwhile, during this dressing down, Wayne was smiling ear to ear.

Strode had become close with Ford during the production of *Sergeant Rutledge*. While making *Two Rode Together*, Strode received word that his mother had died. Strode didn't have the $1,500 he needed to get home and bury his mother. Without equivocation, Ford said, "Go down to the office and tell my son Pat to write you out a check."[20] After the funeral, Ford asked if he was paid back. "You old son of a bitch," Strode said with a smile. "You just took the final payment out of my last check!" Strode's experience with Wayne was unique, in the sense that the actor felt that Ford was guarding his own relationship with the Duke. "Papa was very jealous of his relationship [with Wayne]," wrote Strode in his memoir, "so he put a wedge between us."[21]

While most of *The Man Who Shot Liberty Valance* was shot on soundstages, Ford utilized part of the vast MGM backlot for some of the exterior scenes. The specific part of the MGM property was Lot 3. MGM had several streets that were ideal for stories set in and around the nineteenth century. Just off Overland Avenue in Culver City was Western Street. Aptly named, Western Street "was more elaborate and civilized looking that most Western streets at other studios," which included "frontier-era slat buildings," "a beautifully manicured town square; a tall, steeple-crowned brick courthouse; and a section of railroad track."[22] This part of Lot 3 had an anonymous-looking entrance "insured that the tourists who tended to prowl the perimeter of the other lots were generally absent."[23] Western street was about a mile from the MGM main entrance, which should give readers a sense of how large the MGM studio was. Ford's shooting schedule shows that the company used the MGM backlot for scenes for Shinbone Station as well as the exteriors of Shinbone Street.

The shooting schedule specifies several other scenes as "on location," but details are scant. These scenes include when Tom finds Ranse beaten up, those set near Tom's house (when Hallie visits and when Tom burns it), and the iconic target practice scene where Ranse decks Tom and knocks him on his ass. The *Hollywood Reporter* put John Ford on location at the Canejo Ranch (now Wildwood Park) for five days around October 26th, 1961.[24] The shooting schedule has the company on the MGM backlot on October 26 and on location for the desert exteriors near Tom's house on October 27. Photographs of the Wildwood movie ranch show sets that look near identical to Tom's house.[25]

While finishing up scenes at the Canejo Ranch, Strode recalled when he almost went toe-to-toe with the Duke. During the scene where a drunk Doniphon drives his horse wagon home and sets it on fire, Wayne had trouble stopping the horses. Strode grabbed the reins to help and Wayne knocked him aside. When Wayne fell off the wagon, Strode recalled, "I jumped down and was ready to kick his ass."[26] Ford broke up the confrontation and made Strode cool down for a couple hours. Ford did anything to protect Wayne, Strode remembered. When Ford

Figure 13. Pompey saving Tom from the burning house

hollered for Wayne, "I don't care if his pants were around his ankles, he'd stop and come running."[27] Strode reminded the crew that as much as Wayne may sometime have appeared to be a puppet for Ford, Wayne held nothing but the utmost respect for the man who made his career.

Everyone knew Ford was a cantankerous personality. Those who worked with him and endured his moods frequently spoke admirably about the director. Ford never shot a lot of coverage; he wanted to get the scene right in the shortest number of takes. Film was expensive; this was the reality in which he learned to direct. Some actors found it difficult to work for Ford at first because he sometimes offered little direction for the actors. Lee Marvin found himself wondering what the director wanted at first, before realizing that Ford was giving the actors range, leaving some uncertainty that would work itself out naturally when the cameras were rolling. Jimmy Stewart called this "planned improvisation" that created a "competitive spirit among the actors."[28] Everyone knew, once they got used to Ford's method of "organized tension," that they were "part of something special."[29] Ford did give some direction, when necessary. During the stagecoach holdup, during the first days of shooting, Stewart was unsure about his character motivations for rambling on about the law. Marvin recalled how Ford walked up to Stewart and said, "You are not a coward," and moved back to the camera.[30] After filming, Marvin told Hedda Hopper that Ford is "one of the most intelligent directors I've ever worked with."[31]

It has been argued that the film's final shot, of the train leaving town, may have been from one of Ford's early westerns. However, the shooting schedule does not specify. The entry states, "stock or pick-up" for the scenes of "train going toward Shinbone" and "same train going toward Washington."[32]

Title cards were decided on December 8, 1961. Stewart lost his coin toss for top billing, so John Wayne was given the first title card. Stewart was second, followed by a third card reserved for "a John Ford production" followed by a fourth card featuring Vera Miles, Lee Marvin, and Edmond O'Brien. A total of thirteen title cards were agreed upon, ending with "Directed by John Ford." The final film was approved by the MPAA on January 25, 1961.

The Man Who Shot Liberty Valance was previewed at the March Field Base in Riverside, California, on February 9, 1962. The written audience poll results, all catalogued among the John Ford Papers at the Lily Library, were largely positive; thirty-two "excellent," seventeen "good," nine "fair," and seven "poor."[33] A "very different western," wrote one audience member who thought the film was excellent. Acting was commended across the board; "The best movie I ever saw" was a refrain among those who enjoyed the film. Some responses were clearly attention-seeking or unserious; "I thought that John Wayne was a great, great player," wrote one wag, "and I love him and love his wife and if you ever see him in person tell him he is my favorite actor and I wish to marry him." Even with those who loved the film, several noted that the film had a "slow start" and wished the picture would have been in color.

Even among those who felt this film was simply "good," there were several mentions of how the film should have been in color. Other issues that knocked the film down was that Wayne's character died. Another wrote simply, "bad ending," which is interesting, considering it became one of the most famous and oft-quoted endings in film history. Others were offended by the "trite language" and suggested that producers should "take out all the cuss words." Watching the film in the twenty-first century may make one wonder, "What cuss words?" This is a good reminder that the early 1960s was a transition period between old and new Hollywood and old and new standards of public taste.

The "fair" and "poor" crowd was irked at the ending, like others were, more evidence that the film was a bit ahead of its time or that some audience members were not sophisticated enough when it came to westerns to recognize the master's commentary on the closing of the frontier. Others felt that the film's "fake scenery" and "phony outdoor scenes" looked too much "like TV." A fair criticism, though the obvious stage backdrops add to the film's commentary on the passage of time. The frontier was outdated; so was the appearance of the sets. Some viewers did not like being held in the dark about Tom's cause of death. After decades of narratives tightly focused on John Wayne's every move, it was somewhat radical to have him in a film that was not focused on his character (despite the title pointing to Doniphon). One viewer wrote simply, "What a waste of an evening." "Worst picture of the year," wrote another.

The film's files at the Lily Library also reveal how *The Man Who Shot Liberty Valance* was interpreted around the globe. In Cairo, the title was changed to "The Killer's Secret."[34] Audiences in Egypt also noted that John Wayne "wasn't quite as tough as his reputation calls for." Finnish and German authorities slapped a minimum age limit of sixteen years old for audience members, and Finland made unspecified cuts. Indonesia limited audiences to seventeen years old and over and deleted the scene where Ranse gives Pompey money. Swedish audiences thought highly of the film, though some unspecified cuts were made. When the film premiered at the Skandia Theatre in Stockholm on September 28, 1962, critics raved; "A masterpiece" and "a perfect western" read some of the reviews. Dagens Nyheter wrote that Ford "is keeping the story together with the same superior brilliancy now as he was four decades ago. In American pictures, he is still unsurpassed."

Singapore audiences loved the film but were upset that the movie was not in color, a common refrain among those unsure of the film. When color was all the rage on film and becoming more prevalent on television, seeing such a big motion picture in black and white could make it feel dated. Reports from Singapore suggest that audiences moaned at the opening titles, seeing black and white, which meant the film had to recover "audience favor" during the show. The preview notes suggested that word of mouth would be hampered by the lack of color. Departing viewers were heard saying, "I enjoyed it but what a pity it is in black and white." Authorities in Singapore were also free with the scissors. The stagecoach holdup was shortened, and Valance's line about teaching Ranse "Western law" was cut. The attack on the newspaper was minimized, Peabody's beating was limited by "two strokes," close-ups of the beaten Peabody were cut, and a line regarding "savage redskins" was eliminated. Australian distributors deleted the entire scene where Peabody was attacked.

One lesser known aspect of this film is the popular song titled "The Man Who Shot Liberty Valance," written by Burt Bacharach and Hal David and performed by Gene Pitney. The song stayed on the Billboard Hot 100 for thirteen weeks, topping out at number four in the United States (the song reached number one in Australia). Of course, the song was not used in the film, and there are apparently conflicting accounts of whether it was intended for the film at all. To put any rumor to sleep, *The Hollywood Reporter* provided an update from New York on April 16, 1962, that Gene Pitney was recording a song with Dot Records in conjunction with Paramount Studios (who bought the record company in 1957). Pitney's recording "has been set by Paramount Pictures in conjunction with John Ford's *The Man Who Shot Liberty Valance*, starring James Stewart and John Wayne."[35] The deal was described as part of a promotion, so it's unclear if it was to be used in the film, just the trailer, or for some other kind of promotion. The film was released shortly after this report and the song was subsequently released on its own without direct connection to the film (besides the title and lyrics).

This strange history remains curious, as the song is clearly based on the film/short story's narrative. The best educated guess is that Ford dismissed the song, but the production company had enough money tied into it that they decided to release the song on its own merit. Ford was not accustomed to using new popular music in his films.

6. | Go West, Young Man

Release and Reception

As Joseph McBride documented in his biography of Ford, "Virtually no American reviewers recognized in 1962 that *The Man Who Shot Liberty Valance* was John Ford's artistic summation."[1] Some critics were simply tired of the western, which had been the top genre for decades (as is the superhero genre today, which is beginning to languish in genre exhaustion). Perhaps the flooded market of westerns in the 1950s blinded critics to the fact that Ford's monumental film was more important that they first realized. *Harrison's Reports'* spoiler-heavy review may be one of the only early notices that understood the scope of Ford's vision for the film. *The Man Who Shot Liberty Valance* is "the kind of Western that is part of our history, for its tale was cleaved out of the hard bedrock of so-called fiction and legend that could well have been draped in truths that are beyond disproof."[2] Unfortunately, most critics either didn't understand or were simply too tired of the genre to take the film seriously.

An early review in the *Hollywood Reporter* by James Powers on April 11, 1962, applauded the film as "John Ford's best picture in some years."[3]

Powers strangely categorized the film as "falling generally in the western category," as if there could be any doubt about its membership in the genre. One problem raised in the review was the narrative structure utilizing an extended flashback. Powers didn't quite buy the film's observations on life or history, stating that Stewart's struggle with how he became a prominent politician "is more or less thrown away and, if it were not for the title underlining it, might be lost altogether." While Powers commended the cast and crew, including William H. Clothier's black-and-white cinematography, it's clear that Powers did not fully understand the film's transcendent questions of legend versus fact, though he was not alone in that regard.

Variety ran an early review on the same day calling the film "an entertaining and emotionally involving western," then arguing that it "falls distinctly shy of its innate story protentional."[4] For this anonymous critic, *The Man Who Shot Liberty Valance* may have been a classic in generations past, but in 1962, audiences demanded much more from their films. In other words, Ford's film appeared too simplistic for contemporary audiences. The critic also expressed exhaustion over the genre, writing that "horseback heroes have been climbing out of the living room woodwork for over five years," referring to the numerous western TV shows that aired every week. The *Variety* review claimed that the film was "unconvincing" and the story overwritten, eventually beating the audience over the head with the message. The last twenty minutes were described as "condescending, melodramatic, anti-climactic strokes." Perhaps this critic would have been happier without the script's brilliant line, "When the legend becomes fact, print the legend."

Film Bulletin described the film as "sustaining action" and yet still "disappointing." John Ford was now relegated to elder status as a director of "one-time championship caliber." The critic was clearly hoping for more action, pointing fingers at Ford and company for adapting a short story without enough material for a two-hour film. Even though this review closes by misquoting the film's "write the legend" line, the significance of the words was left hanging in the ether as another reminder that the profound transcendence of Ford's commentary on the history of the genre and frontier myth went over the heads of so many critics.

John L. Scott's *Los Angeles Times* review may be the first to give extended praise to Lee Marvin's Liberty Valance. Scott described Marvin's performance as a "triumph of overstatement" as the actor "etches an evil figure with broad strokes."[5] Scott applauded the rest of the cast and crew but warned audiences that they might find the film "old hat" compared to the "current trend of sophistication," which the reviewer failed to define or elaborate on. Scott also criticized Ford for making parts of the film slow, though those parts were not identified. It is unclear what Scott was expecting of the film, and maybe he was toeing what he saw as the critical line coming from the trade press. Most of the reviews, like Scott's, opened with praise for the film and concluded with often unsubstantiated criticism.

The *Chicago Daily Tribune* made no equivocation, opening the review with this line: "This tiresome Western featuring John Wayne and Jimmy Stewart could have been made of bits and pieces of many of their previous pictures, with all the cliches carefully preserved."[6] Stewart was mocked for being "at his twangiest" in his role as Ranse, the entire cast written off as genre stereotypes and the film itself as "pretty slopping movie making." The review concluded with the most condescending of notes: "Only those who have never seen a movie, or are content to see old movies rehashed, will find much to entertain in this offering." *Photoplay* wasn't much kinder, describing the film as having a "lumbering plot that looks awfully tired."[7]

The *New York Herald Tribune* wasn't sure exactly what to say. The paper's critic admitted that "Ford, as usual, shows how to make a Western really Western," with a common setting that looks brilliantly natural for its characters.[8] The film is understood properly in that the question of who killed Liberty Valance isn't set up as a potboiler (we're all certain it will be John Wayne). Instead, the question regarding Valance is "an element in the drama." In this review, Ford was lightly slapped for his tendency toward "the theatrical, the sentimental" but was ultimately seen as having produced a "delightful" film that will please fans of the director and the genre.

A. H. Weiler's review in the *New York Times* offers the most column inches of any analysis in the first months of release but completely missed the point of the film. Like the others, Weiler commended Ford as a competent director before leaning into criticism of how the "basically honest, rugged and mature saga has been sapped of a great deal of effect by an obvious, overlong and garrulous anticlimax."[9] Weiler questioned why Valance hadn't been killed long ago and asked why Tom would have had any interest in helping Ranse. While Ford "has struck more gold in the West than any other filmmaker," *The Man Who Shot Liberty Valance* "is neither inventive nor intriguing." Completely missing the point of the conclusion and Ford's commentary on the genre, Weiler wrote, "In *Liberty Valance,* there is too much of a good legend."

In May, during the string of lukewarm to condescending reviews, legendary Hollywood journalist Hedda Hopper published a column titled "Ford Keeps Ahead of Young Producers."[10] Hopper reminded readers that Ford had been in the business since he was a young prop man for his brother Francis Ford. Calling *The Man Who Shot Liberty Valance* a "smash hit," she argued that the director "has managed to keep on top when most of the men he started with haven't made pictures in the last decade." Ford's reasoning for his longevity was that he fancies himself as a director, not a producer. He's most at home on set, running the day to day. In fact, Ford mused that "I don't even know what the hell a producer is, and you may quote me on that." Ford did grind one axe in the interview, telling Hopper that the current cycle of films was driven by "moral bankruptcy." Ford's frustration with studios was based on the feedback he'd recently been given. Three studios greenlit projects, only to have the new financiers come back and say there was "not enough sex and violence." "This cycle is vicious," Ford lamented. As we will see in the director's subsequent interviews, the changing tastes found on the big screen would continue to be a source of bitterness and increasing rancor.

Despite some critical pans, *The Man Who Shot Liberty Valance* opened strongly enough. *Hollywood Reporter*'s list of individual theater revenues included $8,061 at the Lyric in Minneapolis, $5,338 at the Rivera in St. Paul, and $8,973 at the Paramount in Buffalo, despite audiences weathering a massive snowstorm. Theaters in Oakland, Lincoln, Rochester, San Francisco, and Philadelphia all reported between $6,000 and $16,000 for the first three days of rentals. For perspective, an average movie ticket cost seventy cents, so making up to $16,000 in a matter of days is impressive.

Trade press reports indicate that the film did well overseas. *Variety* reported that the film did 30 percent better abroad than in the United States and Canada, which grossed about $3 million in rentals by August 1963. *Variety* reasoned that a primary cause for underperformance in the United States was "an overdose of sagebrush sagas" on both film and television.[11] *Variety* reasoned that foreign audiences were drawn to Wayne's portrayal of masculinity as the sole saving grace for overseas audiences. By November, *Hollywood Reporter* shared grosses in Paris alone at $255,300 as well as $13,455 in Madrid's opening week.[12] *The Man Who Shot Liberty Valance* would be one of Paramount's top films in Europe.

Two years after the release of *The Man Who Shot Liberty Valance,* John Ford addressed criticism during an interview with Bill Libby at *Cosmopolitan*. The conversation was predicated on Libby's asking for Ford's defense of westerns, understanding that the genre had come under serious critical disdain. "Every time I start to make a Western," snarled Ford, the critics say, "There goes senile old John Ford out West again."[13] By the 1960s, Ford had dozens of westerns under his belt, "I don't think they need any defense at all." We see similar criticisms today. Scores of both legitimate critics and armchair cinephiles have smeared westerns on social media as inherently simple, racist, sexist, homophobic, patriarchal, and a glorification of toxic masculinity. I wonder how, however, well these critics know the genre. Are they basing their assumptions of that oft-quoted *Playboy* interview John Wayne gave as he was an old, cranky man dying of cancer?

"You're supposed to be an illiterate if you like Westerns," Ford pointed out. "Is it more intelligent to prefer pictures about sex and crime, sex maniacs, prostitutes, and narcotics addicts?" Ford, a product of his era, was naturally put off by films that pushed accepted social boundaries. But Ford was no prude. He worked within the confines of his era, pushing boundaries of his day. Many audiences today may not realize how progressive it was to cast John Wayne as Ethan Edwards, the treasonous, racist, yet deeply loyal family man in *The Searchers*. At the peak of Wayne's fame, when he was unquestioningly accepted as the good guy, Ford pushed the actor to embody a deeply problematic frontier antihero. I have taught *The Searchers* in recent years, and undergraduates are largely amazed at how well this film has aged. For many of them, this is their first western (though our culture has already taught them the prejudices against the genre). Ford's frustration in the years following *The Man Who Shot Liberty Valance* shows us how far back the misconception of the genre dates.

While the director was fed up with the condescending attitude toward westerns, he also understood that critics were piling on the genre out of a desire to be trendy. "Is it more intelligent to prefer a picture simply because it's a foreign film and has subtitles? It may be more fashionable, but it isn't more intelligent." What Ford saw as a prevailing antagonism against the genre is like what we've seen in the twenty-first century. Film historians like Andrew Patrick Nelson have observed that the western has taken on a prestige status; we can see this with films like Jane Campion's *The Power of the Dog* (2021). There is also a range of independent westerns, such as S. Craig Zahler's horror-inspired retelling of *The Searchers* with *Bone Tomahawk* (2015). Filmmakers like Quentin Tarantino can get away with multiple westerns because his spin on the genre gives us something wild and new. The Coen brothers are among the few filmmakers who can remake a traditional, classic western (full disclosure, I prefer the 2010 *True Grit* to the Henry Hathaway film. This is perhaps the one thing Nelson holds against me).

Continuing his commentary on the changing views of the western, Ford argued that "the people who coined the awful term 'horse opera' are snobs."[14] The phrase was found in the *Variety* review of *The Man*

Who Shot Liberty Valance as well as others and was always used in a derogatory manner to describe a group of films that are supposedly old hat. "It's time for those of us who make Westerns, or go to them, or enjoy them in any way, stopped ducking into dark alleys when the subject is brought up. It's time we spoke up." I'm sure anyone reading this book would agree. It is my hope that this volume, as well as the others in the Reel West series can serve as a line of defense against the mischaracterization of westerns.

Despite their reputation as money grabs, westerns were not easy to make. On-location production required sleeping outside, enduring searing desert heat, and dealing with sandstorms—to say nothing of managing cast and crew. Westerns made money because people liked them; Ford reasoned that there should be nothing wrong with that. To the critics who claimed that the western was just too saturated with clichés, Ford rightly countered that this was true of every genre; no type of film was without its stereotypes and narrative shorthand. Ford was frustrated that while westerns were often successful, many people seemed reluctant to admit to watching them. "It's a shame," Ford lamented, "that most persons feel they have to sneak in to see a Western by the side door."

Another issue for Ford—and this is where a generational conflict comes to the fore—is that too many "dirty pictures" were being released. Ford pointedly observed that he didn't "recall a Western which ever had to carry a 'for adults only' sign," something that was becoming increasingly common in the period between the end of the Hays Code and the institution of the ratings system in 1968. Ford was a man of the era when films were declared either appropriate for all audiences or not exhibitable. "After all," Ford joked, "we're not in the burlesque business." Ford said that he was not a prude, but he clearly did not like where Hollywood standards were going. Sure, the western would find new footing with directors like Sam Peckinpah, Arthur Penn, Robert Altman, and Sergio Leone, but it's doubtful that Ford would've enjoyed any of those films if he'd had an opportunity to see them during his lifetime.

Ford offered Libby an insightful, albeit indirect, interpretation of a film like *The Man Who Shot Liberty Valance.* "It is probable that the Westerns have been most inaccurate in over glamorizing and overdramatizing the heroes and villains of the period," said the director, "and in playing up the gunfights." Many critics scoffed at the lack of gunplay and action in *The Man Who Shot Liberty Valance,* something Ford's film does not glamorize. Ford lifts the curtain on the legends of gunfights in frontier streets. In reality, such confrontations were anticlimactic, neither flashy nor stylish but rather sad moments of interpersonal violence. Ford's films are not action oriented in the sense we understand today. Ford's action was included only when it drove the plot and never went on any longer than necessary. For generations who grew up on shootout-heavy westerns, it takes a bit of time to acquire a taste for and an understanding of classic-style westerns.

Ford told Peter Bogdanovich that he saw Wayne as the central character, "the motivation for the whole thing."[15] Ford was not known for his detailed analysis of his own films. When Bogdanovich asked him an essential question about the director's changing view of the frontier, Bogdanovich told Ford, "Your picture of the West has become increasingly sad over the years—like the difference in mood, for example, between *Wagon Master* and *Liberty Valance.*" Ford's quick response was to say "possibly—I don't know—I'm not a psychologist. Maybe I'm getting older." Bogdanovich was right. Ford's films were changing. The differences between *Stagecoach* (1939) and *The Man Who Shot Liberty Valance* are great. While Ford made westerns before and after these films, these two represent the possibilities of the open frontier as well as the closing of the West. Ford was getting older, and so was the genre. Ford could see the evolution, whether he could admit it in an interview or not, and he was the perfect director to weigh in on the changing times.

7. | I Make Westerns

The end of Ford's career came during not only a massive change in American culture but also a shift in critical focus that championed directors in a new way. While American critics could look down their nose at westerns, French critics saw value in directors who found peak form in the genre. Ford, Hawks, Anthony Mann, Samuel Fuller, and many others were adored overseas. The reason was auteur theory. André Bazin's 1957 essay "De la politique des auteurs" noted a trend, evident in *Les* Cahiers du *Cinéma,* the French film magazine that he had cofounded six years prior, to commend the likes of Hitchcock and Hawks, among others, who "appear as almost infallible directors who would never make a bad film."[1] Bazin argued that Ford had a "polemical value" that, with a combination of other means of analysis, "will restore to a film its quality as a work of art."[2] Few directors had a body of work as deep as Ford's, making him an ideal candidate for the booming auteur focus.

American film critic Andrew Sarris brought the French theory to the United States with his seminal 1962 essay "Notes on Auteur Theory." One piece stands out for our purposes here, which is how "the distinguishable personality of the director as a criterion of value" was utilized

Figure 14. Ranse shooting at Liberty, who is falling into the beam

to discuss westerns. Another focus was on a filmmaker's body of work, one that is large enough that critics can identify trends that define both the filmmaker and individual films. Sarris organized his interpretation of auteur theory as containing three circles: technique, style, and meaning. Sarris found value in considering how Raoul Walsh created vulnerability in Bogart's character in *High Sierra* (1941) by using a narrative that questions hypermasculinity.

Pauline Kael, who unjustifiably mocked Sarris, saw auteur critics as "connoisseurs of trash," explaining how auteur theory offers a "theoretical formulation that trash is indeed their chosen province of film."[3] Kael mocked Sarris for liking *High Sierra*, a so-called trash film (Kael would probably be disappointed to learn that it was adoringly restored and released by the Criterion Collection), and derided any kind of authorship study as "intellectual diddling" that justifies "silly movies."[4]

The French critics continued to appreciate Ford, prefiguring a resurgence of Ford. In a 1964 interview with Eric Leguèbe, Ford defined himself first and foremost as an "author of Westerns."[5] Ford may not have appreciated or even known of the growing perspective of great filmmakers as auteurs. One thing is for certain: he would appreciate the admiration and deride the process. "I hate the cinema. But I like making Westerns," Ford said to Leguèbe. "The excitement of the humming of the cameras, and the passion of the actors in front of them, the landscapes on top of that. . . . It takes a huge physical effort to remain lucid and not to fall in the traps of aestheticism and, above all, intellectualism."[6] The only thing Ford hated more about talking about his work was trying to analyze it. Bogdanovich wasn't the only one to get the director's sassy tongue when such questions were asked. When Axel Madsen asked Ford how he decided camera placement, the director sardonically replied, "I say, this is the best shot here, let's put the camera here. You don't do that ahead of time, you do it the day you're shooting."[7] No intellectualism allowed.

The British screenwriter Claudine Tavernier got Ford to describe *The Man Who Shot Liberty Valance* in his own words. "It was a story full of pathos and tragedy," said the director. "I had to fight for seven months to impost it. The banks didn't want it; besides nowadays nobody reads scenarios."[8] Claudine's husband, French director and producer Bertrand Tavernier, also got Ford to talk briefly about *The Man Who Shot Liberty Valance*. Ford was waxing nostalgic about how he knew Wyatt Earp and had heard the supposed real story of the O.K. Corral directly from the man himself as well as Earp's cowboy friends who were all extras in Francis Ford's films when young John was working on them. "*The Man Who Shot Liberty Valance* was based on historical fact, too. It was a fine story," Ford added. "I fought to make it."[9] Ford took his westerns seriously, even if he didn't extend that same courtesy to journalists. The proof is on the screen, in the details found in the stories he told.

In 1967, Peter Bogdanovich published a small book on Ford that compiled interviews and his *Esquire* commentary on the director. The book included Bogdanovich's visit to the set of *Cheyanne Autumn*, an exploration of the director's résumé, an analysis of Ford as a poet and comedian, and a eulogy originally published in *New York Magazine* following Ford's death that was included in the 1978 updated edition. Bogdanovich was probably the first American critic to go all-in on John Ford and went on to produce a documentary on Ford's life and work. Bogdanovich was soon at odds with critics like Pauline Kael, who saw westerns as childish male fantasies. The two would feud over her infamous and embarrassing attempted takedown of *Citizen Kane*. As Bogdanovich recalled in 2020, "It was all an attempt to shoot down the critics who believed in personal films, like me, Andrew Sarris, Eugene Archer, and others. Ironically, she would write as though she were an auteur critic. She kept writing about the directors! She was just full of shit. She had an axe to grind."[10]

Fortunately, even with the rise of the Paulettes (a nickname for the critic's fanatically loyal fanbase), Kael's condescending approach to film appreciation (and westerns specifically) was not embraced by everyone. French critics and historians continued to show interest in Ford. The year before Ford's death, Peter Wollen's 1972 chapter on authorship in his monograph *Signs and Meaning in Cinema* mentioned John Ford specifically. Wollen compares three Ford films—*My Darling Clementine*,

The Searchers, and *The Man Who Shot Liberty Valance*—to highlight how Ford's protagonists navigate the binary conflict of wilderness and civilization. In *My Darling Clementine*, Wyatt Earp moves easily from wilderness to civilization, moving from the "wandering cowboy, nomadic, savage, bent on personal revenge, unmarried, to married man, settled, civilized, the sheriff who administers the law."[11] Writing of *The Searchers*, Wollen argued that "Ethan Edwards's wandering is, like that of many other Ford protagonists, a quest, a search."[12] In *The Man Who Shot Liberty Valance*, we get two characters transitioning in opposing directions. Ranse is helping institute law and order, while Doniphon "has destroyed the only world in which he himself can exist, the world of the gun rather than the book."[13] Understanding this trajectory of characters arcs, culminating with the Westerner no longer being a necessary part of society, makes *The Man Who Shot Liberty Valance* a more powerful film.

The years leading up to Ford's death were full of praise, most famously from Peter Bogdanovich's now classic documentary *Directed by John Ford* (1971). The film has since been reedited and expanded, but at the time of initial release, it was a rare honor. American Film Institute director George Stevens Jr. helped get funding from the California Arts Commission for Bogdanovich's film. Stevens recalled a screening at the Directors Guild where the audience's warm reception "spoke to the test of time. It clarified in my mind the idea of honoring American filmmakers—not for a popular film of a certain year but for a lifetime of enduring work."[14] With many of the world's greatest directors in attendance, "there was laughter and tears and a palpable sense of shared pride on the part of Ford's peers."[15] From within the industry, there was no question where Ford stood among his contemporaries. In the introduction to the

2006 updated version, Bogdanovich tells a story about Orson Welles speaking of the old masters of cinema, followed by simply repeating John Ford's name three times. The 1971 version of *Directed by John Ford* featured many interviews with Ford's collaborators such as John Wayne, Jimmy Stewart, and Harry Carey Jr.

Just months before John Ford died, he was honored with the very first American Film Institute Lifetime Achievement Award. Not only that, but the ceremony also came complete with the Presidential Medal of Freedom from Richard Nixon. Bogdanovich remembered that "a few of the more politically minded [members of Hollywood] protested by *not* coming."[16] He was irked that Jane Fonda, unsurprisingly, picketed outside. "That was her main occupation those days," Bogdanovich wrote of the event, "as well as her privilege, though one might wish she would stop mixing politics with art quite so ferociously."[17] There were certainly reasons to protest Nixon (his work with the House Un-American Activities Committee was damning enough, though Nixon was more focused on bigger fish like Alger Hiss). The AFI event took place just before the Watergate scandal, but this was a night for John Ford. AFI trustee Jack Schneider had just become president of CBS, which helped Stevens lock in *The American Film Institute Salute to John Ford* as a televised event on March 31, 1973.[18]

The celebration was filmed in a conference hall at the Beverly Hilton, and the event was hosted by Danny Kaye. Before the event began, President Nixon and John Ford were introduced and entered together. Ford, in a wheelchair and holding a cigar, remained stoic through a lengthy standing ovation from the audience. The star-studded audience was made up of famous guests and presenters, including Clint Eastwood, Cary Grant, Fred Astaire, Natalie Wood, Charlton Heston, Jack

Lemon, Walter Matthau, Rosalind Russell, Frank Capra, Pat O'Brien, Walter Brennan, Bob Hope, Ronald Reagan (then California governor), Maureen O' Hara, Jimmy Stewart, John Wayne, and host Danny Kaye. "Jack Ford gives us in his work that part of legend and history that might have been lost forever to the American people," Kaye said of the legendary director before introducing John Wayne.

Several of those who knew and worked with Ford recalled their own special nicknames for the director, each personally meaningful, all born of fondness. Wayne called him "coach," probably because Wayne was a football player at USC when the two met. Wayne spoke glowingly of his being part of the Ford stock company, where the regular collaborators with Ford all saw him as a father figure. Wayne playfully introduced a clip of Ford "at his most articulate," entertaining the audience with the famous moment from Bogdanovich's interview when Ford, asked how a scene was filmed, replied, "With a camera." The audience roared. Duke signed off by saying how much he loved Ford, who gave Wayne a big salute while chomping on that cigar.

Jimmy Stewart, who always called Ford "boss," told a story about his first meeting with Ford. Stewart came to his office to discuss the hat he was to wear on *Two Rode Together*. "I think it was a discussion," said a perplexed Stewart as the crowd laughed with him. The camera cut to a rare glimpse of Ford grinning with joy. Stewart had his own hat he wanted to wear, one that was a family heirloom. Ford was won over but suggested that if he was to work with the director again, it would be pertinent to get "hat approval" in the contract. Stewart did work with Ford again, and "in this picture" (*The Man Who Shot Liberty Valance*), "he didn't let me wear a hat at all." Stewart was "fortunate to have been cast under his spell" and what he has learned about his "profession and life."

Another honor came from Jack Lemon, who starred in John Ford's *The Long Gray Line* (1955). Lemon spoke of film being one of America's great native arts that artists should be able to learn by studying under great masters of the craft. Lemon was happy to introduce the AFI's John Ford Fellowship Award, which selected three of five hundred applicants to study at the Center for Advanced Film Studies. Maureen O'Hara, who called Ford "Pappy," sang "Isle of Innisfree" from *The Quiet Man*. The room then sat through a montage of scenes from Ford films, including the diner confrontation in *The Man Who Shot Liberty Valance*, before George Stevens came out to present Ford with his AFI award. The "past and the future have an important connection," said Stevens, who told attendees that the AFI's goal was to celebrate someone whose work has "stood the test of time."

Ford was wheeled to the stage, helped up by Wayne, and walked himself to the podium. The notorious curmudgeon pulled a handkerchief from his jacket and wiped a tear, clearly moved by the outpouring of support for his life's work. The emotional Ford addressed the crowd. "Tonight is the most momentous in the history and the annals of motion pictures. Tonight, for the first time, a chief executive of our nation has honored a public motion picture event with his presence. . . . Thank you, Mr. President." Clearly overcome with gratitude, Ford quickly summarized his emotions and signed off "before I break down."

Before the president took the stage, Kaye summarized the event as "a tribute to the dignity and growth of our profession in that we are all being honored tonight by the presence of the President of the United States." President Nixon felt that Ford would want him to say that this night was not just to honor one man, but that tonight, "we honor a great profession." The president continued, "As an interpreter of the nation's heritage, [Ford] left his personal stamp indelibly imprinted on the consciousness of whole generations both here and abroad" who represents "the best in American films and the very best in America." Again, Ford donned a contagious grin. Afraid he was going to cry, Ford graciously accepted the Presidential Medal of Freedom. Ford was helped from the stage by Charlton Heston and President Nixon. In this time just prior to Ford's death, the director was given the celebration he deserved. The admiration was felt not only in the room that evening but around the nation, with the many fans watching at home.

When Ford died on August 31, 1973, at the age of seventy-eight, he was remembered for the legacy he left to motion pictures. The *New York Times* front-page obituary, however, according the Bogdanovich, "emphasized all the wrong things, called him important for all the wrong reasons."[19] Anyone who watched the AFI celebration would have been curious as to why the *New York Times* called *The Informer* (1935) John Ford's towering achievement. His Academy Awards were listed, of course, but *Stagecoach* and *Young Mr. Lincoln* were listed as "other Ford movies that have won positions on lists of important films."[20] The obituary focused primarily on the director's origins in Hollywood and his films of the 1930s, highlighting also his service in World War II and the fact that he was a bit cantankerous. Any fan of Ford's will be flabbergasted reading the obit. The author, Albin Krebs, who regularly wrote obituaries for the *New York Times,* must have been unable to reach any of the legion of Ford admirers for his piece. Certainly, people who worked on his numerous great films of the 40s and 50s were still around and would have been happy to go on the record about Ford.

What the end of Ford's life shows us today is that he was both admired and misunderstood. Much like today, when Ford, people like

John Wayne, and the entire western genre are often siloed into preconceived (one might argue ill-conceived) notions. As *The Man Who Shot Liberty Valance* has taught us, we must remain simultaneously alert to the legend and the fact. John Ford's legend rests in his days as a film pioneer and his curmudgeon antics. That's not the entire story. His nuanced on-screen storytelling will stand the test of time. Slowly but surely, Ford's legend has been solidified by the facts of his brilliant artistry celebrated by generations since the director's passing. In the fifty years since Ford died, his films have continued to grow in stature. A large part of the celebration is thanks in part to the rise of auteur theory. The next generation of filmmakers would see John Ford as *the* great auteur.

8. | The Legend Grows

In the decade prior to *The Man Who Shot Liberty Valance*, essays appeared that shed light on why the film worked so well (despite what the first critics thought). Robert Warshow's widely cited "Movie Chronicle: The Westerner" (1954) argues that the western hero is at his best with a conflicted moral code, noting that "if justice and order did not continually demand his protection, he would be without a calling."[1] Warshow also believes that the key purpose of the genre is "a certain image of a man, a style, which expresses itself most clearly in violence."[2] Of course, this is exactly what *The Man Who Shot Liberty Valance* comes to question. Ranse departs from the expected rugged individualist trope, doing all he can to win over the town without violence, before realizing he needed violence to defeat just one man. It's a shame that early critics in the United States failed to realize Ford's essential commentary on the film genre he helped solidify.

Building on the groundswell for auteur studies, Jim Kitses wrote *Horizon's West* (1969), one of the first, if not the first, scholarly study on a Hollywood genre.[3] Kitses organized a binary chart showing the conflict between wilderness and civilization that highlights a "shifting ideological play" that "illuminates the genre's basic function, its enquiry into the roots and circumstances of American character."[4] The conflict Kitses outlines applies not only to *The Man Who Shot Liberty Valance* but to all westerns. Conflicts between the individual and the community, nature and culture, and the West and the East all play themselves out in the genre. All three of these, in fact, play out in *The Man Who Shot Liberty Valance*. Ranse's intention to bring law and order to Shinbone hits on many levels. Ranse speaks of social responsibility over self-interest, humanity over savagery, which ultimately will replace an old way of life with a new, more civilized one.

In Kitses's massive chapter on Ford, in which he dedicates lengthy sections to individual films, he showcases the director's talent for "inscribing the opposing forces at play in the American experience and psyche."[5] The western had long explored the nature of rugged individualism, something John Wayne continues to embody for many today, and questions its purpose as times progress. *The Man Who Shot Liberty Valance* is "Ford's profound indictment of that fundamental American virtue; held as an absolute, self-reliance is seen as destructive and ultimately self-defeating."[6] Doniphon's reward for his heroic efforts is life in obscurity and a small funeral for a forgotten man. This rugged individualism is part of the printed legend that Ford's film is pushing up against.

Sure, there were rugged individuals on the frontier, but for society to grow and progress, that way of being had to get stamped out. Part of that process was finding that mythic frontier hero like Tom who has more in common with the savage but is willing to side with the inevitable growth of civilization. When Tom tells Ranse that "Liberty Valance is the toughest man south of the Picketwire, next to me," it's clear that Tom has aligned himself as the rugged individual who is the opposite of everything Ranse represents. Tom and Ranse beautifully personify the binary Kitses explores in *Horizons West*. Tom is the honorable individual who prides himself on his mastery of the brutal landscape, though his love for Hallie helps him understand the importance of the community. Ranse, conversely, embodies notions of social responsibility and an understanding of democracy. He wants to apply the rule of law, but Tom helps him understand that the only way to defeat the likes of Valance is to engage in brutality.

When Kitses interviewed Ford, he asked what drew him to this film. The director's unsurprisingly unspecific response was, "I liked the story . . . two people . . . simple people . . . in a kitchen."[7] Part of this story is simple; perhaps that was the only aspect those first condescending critics could pick up on. Kitses described this kitchen as a "cramped national stage," full of immigrants, a Westerner, an educated Easterner, and a women stuck between it all.[8] Tom is trapped by history, embodying "a contradictory mixture of reactionary values and progressive behaviors," while Hallie picking Ranse over Tom is "not only a choice of self-discovery but also a vote for the values of social regulation. Her sacrifice of Tom accords with the West's march into the future, its phasing out of the individual as guarantor of the law."[9] The dining room, like the kitchen in this film, is a battleground between wilderness and civilization. While Ranse is willing to put on an apron and serve guests, effectively taking on the traditional woman's role to make good on Ericson's hospitality, Liberty Valance works to assert hypermasculine dominance by tripping Ranse and embarrassing him. When Tom steps in to provoke the traditional western standoff, Ranse cannot believe why these two must engage in such a pissing contest.

It is important to point out that there are multiple valid readings of Hallie's picking Ranse over Tom. Some view Tom, who self-destructs and therefore forces Hallie to pick Ranse, as the ultimate tragic hero, working against his own self-interest as he pushes Hallie to go in a direction whose destination is closed to him. However, when I watch this film, I am always taken by Hallie's response to Ranse when he opens the first session of school. She seems completely taken with him from this point on, a moment prior to Tom's demise. This isn't to say that Hallie fell out of love with Tom; she is clearly torn. But it is also fair to say that Hallie made her own decision before Tom burned down the room he built for her. Ford himself saw this film as a story about Hallie, who represents the future—law, order, education, civilization—but it isn't without a yearning for the place lost in that transition.

Kitses argues that *The Man Who Shot Liberty Valance* is a women's film because the entire story hinges on Hallie's decision, a choice that solidifies both her future and that of the country. Perhaps more important that who shot Liberty Valance, is why Hallie began to fall for Ranse in the first place. She desired literacy not only for herself but for others, emphasizing an altruistic nature better suited for a civilized future. It is clear that she loved Tom in a traditional sense—he was, after all, a dominant frontier male—but she saw the future in Ranse. Hallie was as put off by Liberty Valance as Ranse was. Tom, while no friend of Liberty Valance, saw the outlaw as a respected rival. Both Tom and Liberty sit on the same side of Kitses binary, making both men soon to be obsolete. Hallie understood this reality deep down and yearned for a future without savagery. Torn between Ranse and Tom, she chose civilization over wilderness.

Kitses also noted that there were elements of male melodrama at play. Ranse finds his purpose as Tom sacrifices his to solidify Hallie's future. In fact, for Tom, "killing Liberty is killing his own liberty—a metaphysical suicide leading inevitably to the anonymous corpse lying in the wooden coffin."[10] In questioning the very myths that built the frontier narrative, Ford's film explores the conflict between opposing forms of masculinity. This could not have been embodied in any two actors better than in John Wayne and Jimmy Stewart. Both men had played very different types of frontiersmen in previous westerns. Wayne had been the strong, individual frontier hero for most of his career. Stewart, on the other hand, always played the Westerner who was a bit of a fish out of water. Both actors had solidified their version of the frontier character, and by the time *The Man Who Shot Liberty Valance* was released, the power of the film was built on the cultural memory created by Stewart's and Wayne's previous western characters. Bringing Wayne and Stewart together was more than engaging two A-list actors. Both men represented the binary conflict that Kitses used to frame the entire genre.

Lastly, Kitses pointed to Ford's age. Ford was sixty-eight when he made the film, and as others have observed, Ford was an *old* old man. Someone that age today could easily pass as fifty. Ford was a man of the nineteenth century by both chronology and mores. Maybe this is why he was an expert at conveying the past to the present. Selling the frontier to twentieth-century audiences (and twenty-first-century audiences, we might argue, as Ford's legacy continues to gain currency). *The Man Who Shot Liberty Valance* is told from the perspective of Ranse as an old man, a character who could be a stand-in for Ford himself. The director was old and out of place in the modern era. Perhaps this is why Ford always preferred life on the set of a film anchored in the past. He enjoyed the legends and spent a career printing them. However, he also knew that the facts would come out eventually, which is what makes this film such a perfect bookend to the classic era of the western film genre.

In 1970, John G. Cawelti furthered study of the western as part of his attempt to solidify the study of popular culture in higher education. *The Six-Gun Mystique*, which has been revised a couple of times since, aimed to define the western as a cornerstone of popular culture. After all, the western was one of the most prominent cultural genres of the late ninetieth through the first half of the twentieth century. The reason *The Man Who Shot Liberty Valance* works and has found increased prestige over time is that it builds on the generations of frontier lore that the film seeks to critique. Printing the legend is what writers, poets, and filmmakers had been doing all along. Ford knew that that was what he was doing, though he would never say it directly (did he ever say anything directly?). This film is the closest we can get to the director telling us that he knew that Wyatt Earp was printing legends when he came to Hollywood in those early days.

Cawelti outlined the sacrificial nature of twentieth-century westerns, pointing to both *Shane* and *The Man Who Shot Liberty Valance*. In *Shane*, the hero reverts to his gunfighter ways to save the town, but in doing so, foreclosed on his return to the rancher life he hoped to sustain. In *The Man Who Shot Liberty Valance*, Tom "must sacrifice himself and his way of life to save the pioneer leader who will be instrumental in destroying the older anarchical society."[11] Cawelti also highlighted the importance of women in the western, as they are key representatives of civilization. The savagery of the western is almost universally represented by male characters. When Liberty Valance teaches Ranse about "Western law," before beating him to a pulp, the savagery of the frontiersman and the civilized determination of the Easterner could not be more different. Bearing witness to their conflict, Tom comes to understand the need to defend Ranse, which ultimately leads to the sacrifice of his way of life.

The continued relevancy and intrigue of films like *The Man Who Shot Liberty Valance* are fueled by foundational scholars like Cawelti who offered a framework for genre analysis specific to the western. Cawelti outlined three constructive approaches to understanding the western: "ethical," "artistic," and "social and cultural criticism."[12] All three are fully expressed in Ford's film. Cawelti used the ethical framework, as it was a prominent mode of literary criticism. *The Man Who Shot Liberty Valance* is a literary film, in the sense that Bazin described the changing landscape of postwar westerns. Once celebrated, notions of individualism are questioned in this film and shown as outdated. The film also operates on several moral levels. Violence is questioned as a primary means of keeping order.

The artistic structure of the western is also front and center here. While many of Ford's films had showcased, in glorious widescreen, the beauty of Monument Valley, *The Man Who Shot Liberty Valance* is devoid of lavish landscapes. By 1962, Ford's audiences had developed an aesthetic expectation of his films, something that helped define his auteur status. The decision to shoot *The Man Who Shot Liberty Valance* on Paramount soundstages, MGM backlots, and at a local ranch is another signifier of Ford's auteur status. He was conscious of audience expectations (Cinemascope or Technicolor widescreen) and wanted to thwart them, both visually and thematically. The lackluster visuals further emphasize the moral and ethical critiques offered in the film. Taking away the beauty of the frontier helped expose the legend being printed.

When Cawelti wrote his first version of *Six-Gun Mystique*, Freud and Marx were critical darlings who offered frameworks to analyze the culture of masculinity. While cultural and artistic critiques have been oversaturated with the tenets of these two thinkers in the last fifty years, it is easy to see how *The Man Who Shot Liberty Valance* can be interpreted through these lenses. The film offers competing cultures and masculinities. In his updated text, Cawelti explained how "Freud transformed the moralistic conception of wish fulfillment by suggesting that the significant thing about the impulses that found expression in literary form was not their sinfulness but their unconscious character."[13] Valance, Tom, Ranse, and Hallie all harbor subconscious impulses that are exposed through their actions. They represent savagery, frontier heroism, progressive heroism, and community, respectively. The film itself, as stated above, explores Ford's unconscious feelings about the passage of time.

The Marxist critique, Cawelti argued, can "express the ideology or fulfill some ideological need of the social group or class that sponsors, produces or otherwise controls the work."[14] Cawelti highlighted Richard Slotkin's observation that "the decline of myth of the West has created a mythical and ideological crisis in America."[15] Ford's film explores not only the unconscious motivations (Freud) of its characters but also the role that printing the legend had played in constructing power and progress (Marx). The frontier narrative is a perfect landscape to explore constructions of masculinity, individualism, heroism, savagery, and any other form of identity. We may argue that *The Man Who Shot Liberty Valance* is deceptively simplistic. When we begin to unpack the film as a construction of myths and frontier morals, the film's significance appears much greater than at first glance. By calling attention to constructed legends of frontier heroes, all previous frontier narratives come to life in new ways. When I first saw *The Man Who Shot Liberty Valance*, it changed the way I looked at every western I had watched up to that point. In fact, I cannot watch a western without thinking about how it is either printing, questioning, or otherwise engaging some legend.

The Man Who Shot Liberty Valance continued to find cultural traction in the 1970s. The Brat Pack generation of filmmakers like Martin Scorsese continued to treat John Ford as deity. Walter Hill, Martin Scorsese, and Steven Spielberg all offered their admiration in Bogdanovich's updated *Directed by John Ford*. Spielberg recalled seeing *The Man Who Shot Liberty Valance* at a drive-in when his family lived in Phoenix. Spielberg always felt like a "reluctant fighter" like Ranse, and he "related to his moral dilemma." Scorsese remembered seeing *The Searchers* when he was thirteen years old, transfixed with the colorful widescreen. Walter Hill compared Ford ("a Catholic poet") to Dickens, an artist who not only created great works but whose entire output has its own name. Terms like *Fordian* became commonplace to describe themes and visuals regularly found in the director's work. His emphasis on horizon lines and landscapes was coupled with his sentimentality for ethics and morals that define us as people. The beauty and range of human types depicted in Ford films is often compared to a painter with complete command of his canvas.

Dan Ford's biography of his grandfather, *Pappy*, defined *The Man Who Shot Liberty Valance* as "both a Western and a murder mystery."[16] *Pappy* described John Ford as an auteur known for scenes full of beauty and sentiment, but this film is at odds with the director's previous work. The film "is interesting because it is so different," Dan wrote. "It doesn't really look like he made it."[17] Reconsiderations continued into the 1980s.

"For some, the stylization [of *The Man Who Shot Liberty Valance*] is a crippling flaw," wrote Dave Kehr in 1986, "but I find it sublime."[18]

Thanks to a series of considerate Ford biographers, *The Man Who Shot Liberty Valance* continued to attract critical praise, so much so that by now, the early pans of the film seem almost unbelievable. Biographers have not only chronicled the lives of these Hollywood stars but also weighed in on the significance of their life's work. Tag Gallagher offered a twenty-nine-page analysis of *The Man Who Shot Liberty Valance* in his 1986 John Ford biography. Gallagher noted that the film "focuses on the town, as opposed to the range; statehood as opposed to territory, civilization as opposed to wilderness; words (law and education) as opposed to the gun."[19] Seeing everything that the first critics missed, Gallagher depicted the film not as an old-timey horse opera but as a profound statement on "the past as prelude."[20] Gallagher picked out the significance of narrative devices like the cactus rose, the importance of the train as a central metaphor of progress, Ranse's leaning on a wagon wheel (Ford's oft-used symbol of suffering) that impact our view of the film, whether we are conscious of these symbols or not.

Scott Eyman's biographies of John Ford and John Wayne have allowed him to weigh in on *The Man Who Shot Liberty Valance* in 1999 and 2014, respectively. In *Print the Legend: The Life and Times of John Ford,* Eyman picked the book's title from the film, a gesture that highlight's the author's respect for the film. Eyman saw the film as a "memory play" that "focuses on the need to subordinate individual will to a collective struggle for a greater good; unlike many Ford films, *Valance* overtly questions whether the sacrifice is justified."[21] In Eyman's biography of Wayne, the author's perspective remained that the film's mood is that of "overwhelming sadness," because "the men needed to master

Figure 15. Ranse standing next to a sign that says "Vote Statehood"

the wilderness are the same men civilization must expel, and if society is to benefit from the sacrifice, then legend must take precedence over truth."[22] In both books, Eyman chronicled the mostly negative 1962 reception in the United States along with the immediate acceptance of the film as a masterpiece from the European critics.

Probably the most ardent champion of John Ford is critic and historian Joseph McBride, whose 2001 book *Searching for John Ford* is the most extensive study on the director. For McBride, *The Man Who Shot Liberty Valance* is "an allegory of American history. One of Ford's most theatrical pictures," with a "intimate concentration on the performers," offering "a statement of Ford's loss of faith in the ideal of the American frontier," and where "Shinbone seems a dead end."[23] McBride also argued that Hallie's choice of Ranse over Tom was depicted as a "tragic mistake."[24] She does seem melancholy at the end of the film; she did love Tom, but one may also argue that her decision is also an allegory about progress. Her decision to go with Ranse represents her decision of civilization over wilderness. After all, Tom was always reluctant to commit to the future, while Ranse was in full support of social and legal contracts that look forward to the world to come.

McBride's analysis of the film echoes what became the critical consensus by the end of the twentieth century. "Perfectly balancing the genre's irreconcilable contradictions," McBride wrote, "Ford makes a film with a populist thrust but an ultimate skepticism about the values of 'progress.'"[25] McBride also noted how *The Man Who Shot Liberty Valance* is full of references to Ford's previous films (some Gallagher also explores at length), which reminds us that Ford was the perfect filmmaker to make the defining film about the closing of the frontier. McBride explained that not long after the real frontier closed, the western movie genre was born, and John Ford was right there to be a part of it. As McBride and Michael Wilmington wrote in their first book on Ford, "What we are really seeing is not the building of a legend but the gradual stripping away of Stoddard's illusions."[26] In a sense, *The Man Who Shot Liberty Valance* could be one of Ford's most personal films, because through Stoddard, the director is ridding himself of any nostalgia.

In the early 2000s, scholars continued to evaluate *The Man Who Shot Liberty Valance* and its place in the genre's history. Scholars Gaylyn Studlar and Matthew Bernstein edited a collection on Ford's work titled *John Ford Made Westerns: Filming the Legend in the Sound Era*. The subtitle, of course, is a reference to *The Man Who Shot Liberty Valance*. In Charles Maland's essay, the author chronicled the evolution

Figure 16. Tom holding rifle, watching Ranse and Liberty

of Ford from aesthete to the director affectionately known as Pappy. Like Frank Capra and Alfred Hitchcock, Ford's reputation as an auteur grew as critics began to assess his body of work, particularly his westerns. Maland and others have argued that "Ford's vision is perhaps best expressed through his Westerns."[27] Ford was able to toy with legends of the Wild West in everything from the taming of the West epic *The Iron Horse* (1924) to the frontier "road film" *Stagecoach* (1939), all the way through *The Searchers* (1956). As Andrew Sarris wrote in his review of *The Man Who Shot Liberty Valance*, "The legends with which Ford is most deeply involved . . . are the legends of honorable failure, of otherwise forgotten men and women who rode away from glory toward self-sacrifice."[28] This is embodied in no one more accurately than in the character of Tom Doniphon, who sacrifices his way of life, and the love of his life, for the sake of progress.

British scholar David Lusted viewed *The Man Who Shot Liberty Valance* as an anachronism for the West, where "the man of the West whose way with a gun excludes him from the civilized society he helped create."[29] The elegiac film highlights the indifference of the passage of time. Shinbone goes on, but the cost of progress weighs on the town's old timers. Lusted drew comparison to *The Shootist* (1976), another film where Wayne, here playing gunslinger and former sheriff J. B. Books, personifies the closing of the frontier and perpetuation of its mythos. Books, like Doniphon, is the last of his breed, soon to be a relic of a time gone by. Both characters are conscious of the inevitability of progress and can clearly hear their relevancy timeclock ticking its final seconds.

In another volume, Patrick McGee compares *The Man Who Shot Liberty Valance* to films like *High Noon* and *Rio Bravo* in how they chastise fascistic brutality. In Ford's film, "Liberty Valance symbolizes the use of raw physical force to justify a socioeconomic structure that privileges wealth at the expense of the common man."[30] Liberty Valance is quite possibly the nastiest villain in all of Ford's work. The cruelty of the frontier has only become more pertinent with time. The twenty-first century has seen a reckoning of sorts with toxic masculinity, for which Liberty Valance is a poster child. Ranse and Tom represent two different kinds of common men, useful in different historic periods. The film shows us a transition period, when the viciousness of Tom was needed to defeat Liberty, so that men like Ranse could prevail.

Doniphon's sad, desolate send-off leaves Ranse and Hallie melancholic over their life journey that led to a good man's having to die alone. McGee argued that "*The Man Who Shot Liberty Valance* is probably the most pessimistic Western ever made, one that borders on nihilism."[31] As McGee and others have pointed out, Ford does in fact print the fact while making a commentary on printing legends. Ford's view of how legends are made is gloomy, but to call it nihilistic may be inaccurate. Liberty Valance is a nihilist, to be sure, but the film's poetic summation of the frontier mythos displays the necessary acceptance of law and order (a truly anti-nihilistic stance). As an old man, Ford himself was conscious of the time that had passed, and while he yearned to sample that time again, he also fully understood the necessity of moving forward. There was something majestic about the frontier, which Ford captured in his amazing shots of Monument Valley. However, there was also a constant danger surrounding everyone in the lawless frontier years. The American West is doubtless littered with unmarked graves of victims of the likes of Liberty Valance. Nostalgia for such a time is shattered by Valance's bullwhip.

The Man Who Shot Liberty Valance was chosen for preservation in the United States National Film Registry by the Library of Congress in 2007. A sure sign of the film's ongoing appreciation, critics and historians have continued return to it as a source worthy of new analyses and reflection. In 2009, Richard Brody wrote in *The New Yorker* that the film is "both the most romantic of Westerns and the greatest American political movie."[32] The struggle to institute rule of law is only one element of the film, which Brody rightfully saw as a deeply political narrative. Part of Ranse's struggle is to get the community to participate in a democracy. Intimidation by the Valance gang rode roughshod over any fair political process. The film encourages us to consider a time when fair elections in our country were not a given.

In 2011, film critic Roger Ebert described the film as "pensive and thoughtful," representing "fascism against democracy" and addressing "the tyranny of the strongman over the ordinary people."[33] Ebert also highlighted the important fact that Shinbone appears to be the only western town that doesn't have a brothel. This is an important genre stereotype that Ford leaves out of this film, yet another sign of the imminence of Shinbone's progress. Echoing Brody's claim about *The Man Who Shot Liberty Valance* as a political film, Ebert pointed to the film's exploration of "the role of a free press, the function of a town meeting, the debate about statehood, the civilizing influence of education."[34]

Part of the film's growing stature is the role of Pompey, which was both strong and timely. Woody Strode, who helped break the color barrier in professional football, was not a strong character in an important film at the height of civil rights debates. Having already starred in Ford's race-centered courtroom drama *Sergeant Rutledge,* Strode's Pompey is Doniphon's support system in the film, the one who procures the gun with which Tom Doniphon kills Liberty Valance. As Abigail Horne observed in her 2012 essay "The Color of Manhood," "Pompey is not only a sturdy version of masculinity in a film that troubles masculinity at every turn; Pompey is also a sturdy version of an American in a film that troubles the story of America itself."[35] Although Strode's character was largely dismissed in several studies, Horne noted that Ford biographer Joseph McBride gave Pompey a more vital read, comparing him to the contemporary Black man of the Jim Crow era (secondary but yet essential).

Pompey doesn't balk at the prospect of changing times, perhaps because progress may also help him take more agency in the world. He gets a seat in Ranse's classroom, where he tries to recite the Constitution's

Preamble, forgetting the important line "all men are created equal." "A lot of people forget that part," Ranse tells Pompey. Shortly after, Tom breaks in and rips Pompey from the school, citing education as a waste of time. Despite previous scholars' seeing this scene as one placing Pompey in a master/slave situation, Horne argued that when Pompey is reminded that "all men are created equal," he is standing in front of an image of Lincoln, in which "Ford aligns Pompey with the emancipation of black men, not their enslavement."[36] In a film about the death of the old and the promise of the new, it makes sense to see Pompey as integral to the progress that Ranse is fighting for. The film's release in 1962 came after years of battles for racial integration in schools and President Eisenhower's Civil Rights Act of 1957 (protecting voting rights for minorities) and just two years before President Johnson signed the Civil Rights Act of 1964.

Ford emphasized progress through *The Man Who Shot Liberty Valance* in other ways as well. In her 2016 study on Wayne and Ford, Sue Matheson explored the influence of Victorian novels on "Ford's views of gender and community, self-sacrifice on the part of the individual, and death in his movies."[37] This observation helps us understand why Ford would have felt the passage of time so strongly, as he was not only feeling his own clock ticking but also how far time had evolved from the Victorian era. Regarding *The Man Who Shot Liberty Valance*, Matheson aptly pointed to the importance of hats. The age-old white-hat/black-hat trope is instituted when Doniphon shoots Valance. Doniphon dons a white hat as his aims his rifle at Valance. Ranse, conversely, has no hat, which can signify that his importance is beyond the realm of the old cowboy yarns. Matheson also highlighted the film's brief commentary on race, noting that just before Doniphon breaks up the classroom and

Figure 17. Pompey with the photo of Lincoln in the background

takes him away (a nod to post–Civil War bondage), Pompey forgets the word *equality* when he recites the Declaration of Independence. Lastly, Matheson, like McBride, saw Hallie's story as a "metaphorical cross to bear," as she is clearly not happy with her life married to a US senator.[38]

In Nancy Shoenberger's book on the relationship between John Wayne and John Ford, the author drew a useful connection between Ford's *Stagecoach* and *The Man Who Shot Liberty Valance*. Three actors from *Stagecoach*—John Carradine, John Wayne, and Andy Devine—are also present in *The Man Who Shot Liberty Valance*, which Schoenberger argued "consciously completes the full circle of his historical and mythological frontier saga."[39] Another useful question is asked, which is why wouldn't Doniphon set the record straight? Schoenberger rightly reasoned that it is because "heroes don't brag. It would have been unsporting of him to seize Stoddard's glory, no matter the truth of the situation."[40] Tom remains the hero, and Ranse is forced to carry the weight that his success is based on a lie. Tom kills Valance from a protected position (not a fair fight by frontier rules), but he can live with it. Ford's film, of course, ultimately forces us to realize that history is made up of these kinds of stories. The legend is often printed, and the inconvenient facts are siphoned away.

On the film's sixtieth anniversary, *The Guardian* published a celebration of *The Man Who Shot Liberty Valance* by Oliver Macnaughton. It should be stated that while the film was first appreciated by European critics, it should not surprise anyone that the most comprehensive anniversary piece came from a European publication. Macnaughton had high praise:

> *The Man Who Shot Liberty Valance* is not a film about American heroes but about the country itself. Ford brilliantly captures this through the personas of its two leading actors that were cultivated over the preceding decades. He's self-critical of both his own legacy as a film-maker and the country that he helped mythologize. If *The Great Gatsby* is the great American novel, then this is the great American film.[41]

Macnaughton perfectly captured how many of us feel about this film. It represents everything that historians and critics have mined from its story, but the film also can transcend all of it. The film is about America. It is about how we tell stories, and the emotion in the film expands well beyond the genre; sometimes, the legend is "no longer worth printing."[42] In *The Man Who Shot Liberty Valance*, Ford both prints the legend and lifts the veil and exposing the truth. The film has stayed with me primarily for this reason: when we explore history, we must be aware of the legends and lies that may have brought us there in the first place. The problem of legends comes up constantly when studying Hollywood history. We know that memoirs are often fun but frequently self-fulfilling prophecies. Some writers and historians are also fallible and can be attention seeking in their work by doing intellectual gymnastics to create controversy. The rest of us are in the middle, sifting the stories for facts buried underneath legends.

9. | Printing the Legend as Mythology

I have been privileged to co-teach, with my philosophy colleague Mark Peterson, an ongoing course on superheroes as modern mythology. Mark and I use the genre study as a conduit to explore modern mythology, ultimately using Joseph Campbell's exploration of the hero's journey to define and make meaning out of our own lives. As our course evolved, we began to incorporate into it other elements of popular narrative, and when I began writing this book, we used *The Man Who Shot Liberty Valance* as a discussion point. This chapter grew out of a series of conversations with students, very few of whom had seen the film but were nonetheless intrigued by the idea of printing legends.

The transitional period from the Western frontier to twentieth-century civilization is not unlike the lightning-fast evolution we've seen from analog to digital technology over the last quarter century. Cultures changed, lives changed, and standards changed, and our entire way of being has been altered. Seemingly, everything is different from when I was a child in the 1980s. Even my students, born in the late 90s and early 2000s, have seen their share of major shifts in our world, and as in *The Man Who Shot Liberty Valance*, we are all, in our own ways, subject to a

Figure 18. Ranse looking at the cactus rose on Tom's coffin while Hallie stands outside the door

longing for the past. Even in the face of the radical changes to popular culture propelled by the streaming era, there is still a market for theatrical film, vinyl records, polaroid cameras, and other forms of analog technology. The past is always alive in the present, which we also see in *The Man Who Shot Liberty Valance*—a longing for the past, a desire to progress, and an awareness that time inevitably marches on.

The Man Who Shot Liberty Valance is not only a transcendent western; it is also a film that transcends Hollywood's golden age. While Ford was waxing melancholic about times gone by (his own and the frontier's), many have viewed the film through the lens of the director's favorite genre. However, with the film coming out in 1962, as the dust was settling after the collapse of the old Hollywood studio system, the story can also feel like an elegy for Hollywood itself. This elevates the

Figure 19. Tom, holding match with flame, telling Ranse that it was he, not Ranse, who killed Liberty

film further, adding to its mythological status as a great American work of art. As twentieth-century thinker Joseph Campbell once said in a 1981 lecture, "In our society of fixed texts and printed words, it is the function of the poet to see the life value of the facts round about, and to deify them, as it were, to provide images that relate the everyday to the eternal."[1] The plights of the frontiersman and the future-oriented characters in *The Man Who Shot Liberty Valance* set up something equally timeless, as it is time stamped. In this concluding chapter, I will utilize Joseph Campbell's mythologically structured hero's journey to showcase how Ranse Stoddard takes on a classic trajectory that adds truth and relevancy to his character. Using this framing, this chapter will seek to explain the enduring relevance of *The Man Who Shot Liberty Valance*.

The mythology of the hero's journey was popularized when George Lucas applied Campbell's framework to Luke Skywalker in *Star Wars: A New Hope* (1977). Lucas read Joseph Campbell's *The Hero with a Thousand Faces* (1949) and was transformed. Lucas did the same with Indiana Jones, having created the iconic character of the popular Steven Spielberg franchise. These characters work, and are popular, for very specific reasons that track with thousands of years of mythological storytelling from across the globe. Luke Skywalker and Indiana Jones are not only larger-than-life characters but also inhabit a grounded sense of humanity that we can all relate to. Hollywood story consultant Christopher Vogler wrote that he "came to believe that the Hero's Journey is nothing less than a handbook for life, a complete instruction manual in the art of being human."[2] Vogler was right, as Campbell taught us that the essence of our own journey is following our bliss.

Campbell studied global religious texts and found a similar trajectory in the journeys of many spiritual and mythological figures across historical and geographical lines. Campbell began to see a universal story that applied across the spectrum of global myths, something that could be applied to our own lives. He found that myths are the dreams of the culture; myths are symptomatic of the psychological processes of a culture. These processes are rites of passage that encapsulate the hero's journey. In *The Hero with a Thousand Faces*, Campbell wrote, "The hero . . . is the man or woman who has been able to battle past his personal and local historical limitations to the generally valid, normally human forms."[3] In other words, the hero's journey puts us (the reader/viewer) into relation with the surrounding world and our place in it. When Ransom Stoddard finds fame and notoriety for killing Liberty Valance, despite what really happened, Ranse moves past personal limitations to become something bigger than his abilities would allow while fumbling a pistol. There would be no Senator Stoddard without willingness to be a part of the legend. Only after completing his journey did Ranse acknowledge the truth of the event that defined his life, a story that Tom took to his grave.

For Campbell, the hero is "eloquent, not of the present, disintegrating society and psyche, but of the unquenched source through which society is reborn."[4] The town of Shinbone, like the rest of the frontier, was in the process of becoming modernized, or reborn, as a place of law and order. A civilized future was facing a history of frontier justice. Campbell argued that "The hero has died as a modern man; but as eternal man—perfected, unspecific, universal man—he has been reborn."[5] Ranse, while still of this world at the end of the film, has become just such an eternal man, immortalized as the man who shot Liberty Valance. Even when he offers the real story, one that implicates himself as a phony of sorts, the legend is too large to topple. The legend remains printed because it has become eternal.

The hero's journey comprises twelve steps, slightly simplified by Vogler in how he applied them to popular film. We can see how Ranse closely follows this arc. Each stage is variably essential depending on the hero and depending on whether the journey is successful or complete. Vogler's summation of Campbell's mythological deep dive is as follows:

1. Ordinary world
2. Call to adventure
3. Refusal of the call
4. Meeting with the mentor
5. Crossing the first threshold

6. Tests, allies, enemies
7. Approach to the inmost cave
8. Ordeal
9. Reward (seizing the sword)
10. The road back
11. Resurrection
12. Return with elixir

Vogler's outline offers a watered-down version of Campbell's erudite breakdown of world mythology, giving us a template with which to overlay the hero's journey onto popular culture. The following analysis of *The Man Who Shot Liberty Valance* will utilize both Vogler's outline and Campbell's perspective of the relevant details as they apply to the film. In his book *Myth and the Movies*, Stuart Voytilla opens his chapter on westerns and mythology by citing *The Man Who Shot Liberty Valance* ("When the legend becomes fact, print the legend"). Movies, specifically westerns, are "American mythology," argues Voytilla, "the dime novel propagated the legends, a pulp version of the Greek Homer weaving tales of Wyatt Earp and Billy the Kid, transforming good guys and bad into epic heroes."[6] Tom Doniphon and Ransom Stoddard are two legendary characters who embody the history of the western genre as well as the history of the frontier itself. Their opposing trajectories work toward the same goal—a better future.

The hero's journey is transcendent. The hero is reborn as an immortal figure who represents something beyond themselves. Campbell argued that "it has always been the prime function of mythology and rite to supply the symbols that carry the human spirit forward, in counteraction with those constant human fantasies that tend to tie it back."[7] Campbell's hero's journey includes a separation, an initiation, and a return that serve as the backbone of the journey. Campbell saw all traditions, religions, and legends as mythological. The goal of their mythology is to put us in touch with our surrounding world. Frontier mythology operates the same way, be it consciously or unconsciously, as the genre regularly puts us into relation with the real frontier, actual lived history and its implications, as well as in dialogue with the nature of heroism. *The Man Who Shot Liberty Valance* includes many of these mythological components, something that makes the film stand out from the genre and stand the test of time.

THE HERO'S JOURNEY

The Man Who Shot Liberty Valance is primarily a flashback to 1910 from a time twenty-five years hence, as Senator Ransom Stoddard (James Stewart) and his wife, Hallie (Vera Miles), recount how the senator won favor in the small town of Shinbone, Arizona. Ranse and Hallie's train pulls into a modern Shinbone. The frontier has been settled, and Arizona and New Mexico have been states since 1912. Forty-eight states have joined the Union, and the binary between wilderness and civilization is now barely noticeable. A journalist asks Senator Stoddard for an interview, not sure why the famed politician is in town. Meanwhile, Link (Andy Devine), the old town sheriff, takes Hallie on a ride out to the desert. They visit the home of Tom Doniphon, her old flame. They notice the burned home surrounded by beautiful cactus roses, which will become an important symbol in the film.

While Ranse, Hallie, Poppey, and Link are mourning beside Doniphon's coffin, the journalists barge in, demanding a story. Whom was the esteemed senator here to mourn? Why doesn't anyone know who Tom

Figure 20. Link, Hallie, Pompey, and Ranse sitting beside Tom's coffin

Doniphon was? Reluctantly, Ranse tells the newspaper about the town before the arrival of the railroad, when he first came to Shinbone. Ranse took journalist Horace Greely's advice literally, to "go west, young man . . . seek fame and fortune!"[8]

The ordinary world for Ranse is something we don't see in the film; we are only led to believe that it exists for our hero from the civilized East Coast. We meet Ranse while he is on his way from the ordinary world to the world where his heroism will be solidified. His call to adventure was taking Greely's advice. Campbell refers to this stage as "separation," when the hero crosses the first threshold. We meet Ranse as he crossed that line from East to West and into the frontier. Ranse takes the call but backs down quickly upon meeting Liberty Valance. This could be interpreted as a brief refusal of the call, though Ranse

Figure 21. Liberty Valance outside the bar looking at Ranse

appears even more motivated in his mission once he becomes a victim of frontier violence.

As soon as Liberty Valance enters the scene and beats Ranse, the hero has entered the "belly of the whale," as Campbell calls it, which is the first big obstacle or let-down (in *Star Wars,* this is the literal trash compactor on the Death Star). Ranse is gleaming with optimism—"Go west!" he was told—and suddenly, he is at the business end of Valance's whip. When the Valance gang steals a female passenger's jewelry, Ranse stands up for her. When Ranse identifies himself as a lawyer, Valance beats him unconscious to teach him about "Western law."

Doniphon finds Ranse and brings him to safety and aid in Shinbone. This pivotal moment for a newly minted lawyer motivated the future senator to find a way to establish law in this frontier town. The problem is that most citizens of Shinbone rely on Tom Doniphon, a perfect example of Warshow's Westerner, to handle the town's problems with intimidation, fists, and if necessary, guns. While Tom and Ranse see different paths to a future, Ranse must learn the ways of the frontier that must be defeated if rule of law is to be practiced in Shinbone. This relationship between Tom and Ranse is one of mentorship. The clash between law and frontier justice is apparent, as Tom says, "Out here a man settles his own problems." Ranse cannot take on Valance by himself. As Tom teaches Ranse, "Liberty Valance is the toughest man south of the picketwire . . . next to me."

Ranse begins his initiation as he settles into town. This process includes a "road of trials," as Campbell calls it, or a series of tests, allies, enemies (step six of the hero's journey). Ranse must find a way to establish law, especially after learning that Shinbone's sheriff, Link Appleyard, is uniquely inadequate to handle Liberty Valance. Ranse helps at the local restaurant as his health improves (all his money was stolen in the stagecoach raid, so he wants to earn his keep). It is here that Ranse learns about the social side of town, as Tom brings Hallie a cactus rose. The romance between them is clear, something that will become threatened if Ranse's image of progress were to occur. Hallie is naturally drawn to the frontiersman; it was the safe choice in a lawless land. However, the frontier will soon close, and the future was upon them.

Ranse's initiation is also full of self-realization, or apotheosis. When Ranse is waiting tables (seen as a woman's job), Liberty Valance enters the restaurant and snickers at Ranse. Valance trips Ranse, who drops a plate with its juicy steak. The plate was destined for Tom, who stands up, and Valance returns to the standoff in a display of frontier hypermasculinity. At this moment, Ranse proves who he is as he cannot

Figure 22. Ranse, with gun, after Liberty shoots the pot next to Ranse's head

believe these two are willing to kill each other over a steak. Ranse picks recovers the steak from the floor and slams it on the table in disgust. Campbell calls this a "perilous journey into the darkness by descending . . . into the crooked lane of his own spiritual labyrinth."[9] Ranse went west and quickly encountered a world and its creatures that were quite different from his own. Campbell also adds a psychological component, influenced by Jungian archetypes, whereby the hero will encounter mythological opponents. Both Doniphon and Valance are quintessential frontier archetypes. They are different sides of the same coin, driven by individual toughness (though Valance has a gang), a mentality focused on physical strength, and pride in one's ability to survive in the wilderness of it all.

Another trial comes as a reminder from Dutton Peabody, founder of the *Shinbone Star,* who tells Ranse that "you can't shoot back with a law book." Regardless, Ranse hangs his law sign at the newspaper and refuses to get himself a gun. This begins what Campbell refers to as a "process of atonement," during which the hero merges with his truly identity. Ranse sees himself as a lawyer, but he needs to be more than that if he wants to succeed in his mission. Peabody and Ranse begin to gather news and information about the territory. The newspaper will be an ally in Ranse's fight for progress, helping more people become literate and informing them of their power (as voters, for example, who can use their understanding of government to have a say in their surroundings).

Through this process, Ranse learns that Hallie, along with many others in the territory, is illiterate. Ranse seeks to use his position to spread education. By teaching the community to read and write, he will bridge the gap between the old and new world. Ranse writes on the chalkboard, "Education is the basis for law and order." More people arrive every day, excited to learn. Ranse knows that an educated populace will know both how and why to utilize their voice and vote to establish a democracy. Naturally, Ranse uses the local newspaper as the course textbook.

As a territorial statehood election arrives, Ranse begins to approach the inmost cave. Ranse has convinced his town to use its collective voice, which works wonders until Valance shows up to intimidate voters to insert Valance as a delegate to Congress. Ranse attempts to convince Tom to offer service as a delegate, knowing that Valance wouldn't stand against him. Even though Tom refuses, Ranse and Peabody are elected

Figure 23. Ranse teaching from his desk

delegates. In retaliation, Valance and his gang burn down the newspaper building and beat Peabody brutally. At this point, Ranse realizes that a man like Valance speaks only one language—violence. In this world, bullets speak. Ranse begins to practice target shooting with a revolver, a famous scene in which Tom embarrasses Ranse by outshooting him as he stands under cans of white paint that spill over him. Ranse has a moment of final apotheosis when he slugs Tom, who lands on the ground. Ranse has become both a frontiersman and an educated Easterner. Ranse arrived with a mask of a lawyer but has now become a version of the rugged individual capable of asserting dominance. Once dominance over bullying is attained, he can finally enact law and order on the frontier. During this process, Hallie begins to fall for Ranse, a sign that current changes may be permanent.

Figure 24. Ranse shooting the gun next to Tom

When Ranse decides to take on Valance, he sees what Campbell calls the "ultimate boon." He now knows what must be done to civilize the West. Vogler calls this the "final ordeal." Even though Tom eventually taught Ranse how to shoot with proper balance and a slow squeeze of the trigger, Tom knows that Ranse is too much of a greenhorn to take on Valance. Still lacking skill, Ranse shows strength and determination to defeat Valance. When Valance stumbles out of the saloon, Ranse stands ready to do away with frontier bullies once and for all. Valance toys with Ranse, shooting a hanging pot next to his head before shooting the gun from his hand. As Ranse lifts the gun and fires, Valance falls to the ground, dead. Of course, as we soon learn, the death shot came from Tom, who was standing in the back with a rifle. Tom knew what had to happen, that Ranse had to win, but knew that he couldn't do it alone. The future was with Ranse, Tom knew, which is why he never revealed the real story about who shot Liberty Valance. Understanding that times were changing and the need for people like Doniphon was dwindling, he gets drunk and burns down his home, including the room he was building for Hallie, who is destined to be with the man of the future, not the man of the past.

Building on his newfound frontier credentials, coupled with his lofty Eastern ideals, Ranse can begin the next step in his hero's journey, the return. He takes his place in public office (the "reward," as Vogler calls it) and goes to Washington in a position to enact real progress to civilize the frontier. Vogler also refers to this part of the Journey as the "road back and return with elixir." In the film, the flashback ends, and we are back to modern day. Ranse tells the new editor of the *Shinbone Star* the real story, that he didn't shoot Liberty Valance, and that he is therefore a fraud. The editor replies that he would not run the story, because "this is the West, sir. When the legend becomes fact, print the legend." At this point in the journey Campbell views the hero as a master of two worlds. Ranse has achieved this as he has had a successful career in Washington, while also retaining his own image as a frontier hero. Even Hallie can see the two worlds. She still has love for Tom, as evidenced the cactus rose that she places on his coffin. However, she also reminds Ranse that the frontier that was once a wilderness has become a garden.

As Ranse and Hallie take the train back to Washington, the conductor is making sure everything is comfortable for the senator. As he walks away, he says "Nothing is too good for the man who shot Liberty Valance." It's clear that Ranse has reached immortal status. Even he cannot change his image at this point. His story transcends his own life. Ranse has completed the classic hero's journey, one that pre-dates the

Figure 25. Mr. Scott tearing up the story Liberty Valance told him

American frontier and will continue to live on long after the frontier's settlement. In fact, Campbell argued that "a good life is one hero's journey after another."[10] Ranse's victory over Valance and subsequent election was one such journey. His time in Washington would certainly produce calls to adventure for future journeys. Ranse does promise Hallie that they would return to the West, but of course, that does not happen for many years. Arrival was too late to reconnect or reconcile with Tom, which is why the funeral had an extra layer of sadness.

We may also argue that while Ranse is the hero in the sense that he helped make the frontier safe from killers like Liberty Valance, it is important to recognize Tom's role in that victory. He was a martyr. Tom likely had many previous journeys in which he would have been the central hero. The frontier era was full of communities, caravans, and

Figure 26. Liberty taking Ranse to task in front of Tom after the election

territories that needed Tom Doniphon types. For Campbell, the return could take multiple forms—death or departure. "Here the whole sense of the life is epitomized," observed Campbell.[11] Ranse's return is one of departure, from Shinbone to Washington, which allows him to make real change. Tom's return is one of death, wherein he is transformed, at least for the few at the funeral, into a "synthesizing image."[12]

What the hero's journey in *The Man Who Shot Liberty Valance* can teach aligns with what Campbell offered as a lesson: "All these myths that you have heard and that resonate with you, those are the elements from round about that you are building into a form in your life."[13] The western genre has been a resonant form of popular culture since the frontier era. The myth-making began immediately. People have been reading and creating mythologies around the frontier that continue

Figure 27. Ranse and Hallie on the train, looking melancholy

making its struggles, adventures, and personalities engaging for future generations. *The Man Who Shot Liberty Valance* offers us an elegy for the Wild West while also presenting the struggles that occur during transition points in history. The passage of time is something we all experience, along with the accompanying emotions (excitement, despair, nostalgia, regret, surprise, happiness, and so on). By setting the film at the end of the frontier era, John Ford offers a film that is both set in time and place while remaining eternally timeless. This is but one example of many that showcase how the western can retain an everlasting presence in our popular imagination.

10. | The Western as Immortal

The Man Who Shot Liberty Valance came out during a period of transition in Hollywood cinema and is, in fact, about a period of transition. Campbell reminded us that "myths do provide role models for that society at a given time. What that mythic image shows is the way in which the cosmic energy manifests itself in time, and as the times change, the modes of manifestation change."[1] The definition of the frontier molds itself to contemporary mores. The western, of course, is often situated in the American Southwest. But it can also be found across the globe and even in space. In Hollywood, John Ford made his West in Monument Valley. In Japan, Akira Kurosawa, a dedicated fan of John Ford's westerns, brought the frontier narrative in line with samurai mythology. Italian filmmaker Sergio Leone used the lone gunfighter narrative in his Italian westerns (which were shot in Spain). The *Star Trek* TV series and subsequent films branded space as "the final frontier." George Lucas also took the western into outer space for his *Star Wars* franchise, with Han Solo representing a brand of rogue gunfighter. While the western has had and continues to see a global impact, the genre has deep roots in American popular culture.

As film historian and cohost of the *How the West Was Cast* podcast Andrew Patrick Nelson argues, journalists and historians love to write about the western being dead just as much as they enjoy writing about its resurgence.[2] However, this ebb and flow is part of a predictable life cycle that has kept the genre alive for over a century. The origins of the frontier narrative on our public consciousness dates to 1845, when John L. O'Sullivan coined the term *manifest destiny* in an essay about America's perceived right to expansion. As the Wild West came to an end and the frontier became settled, Frederick Jackson Turner introduced his "frontier thesis" in 1893 in a speech before the American Historical Association. Turner hit on the binary conflicts that make the western as a mythological place so engaging. The frontier, as he defined it, saw "the meeting point between savagery and civilization."[3] This timeless conflict has kept the western genre relevant for over a century.

The archetypal characters in *The Man Who Shot Liberty Valance* represent the western genre in 1962 as much as they embody the real constellation of people who were present as the frontier was settled. Ranson Stoddard, Tom Doniphon, and Liberty Valance also bear resemblance to characters in the genre before and after the film was released. These characters are mythological, something that makes them timeless. As Campbell argued, "Myth is not the same as history; myths are not inspiring stories of people who lived notable lives. No, myth is the transcendent in relationship to the present."[4] *The Man Who Shot Liberty Valance* is not history, of course. It is an interpretation of history through the lens of archetypal figures. These characters transcend both history and popular culture genre to achieve immortality.

One could make a similar argument about the star image of Wayne and Stewart. These actors were people, but they were also stars, something that had a different cultural meaning in 1962. The casting of each actor brought with it the baggage of previous films. They were playing new characters but were also shouldering the history of their prior roles. The film would not have played the same if Tom had been played by Stewart and Ranse by Wayne. The characters aligned with the history of their respective careers and, therefore, representing much more than an individual film.

By 1962, Hollywood production was nothing like the decades prior, and attendance was a far cry from its peak in 1946. However, one of the most popular films of the decade was a western, *Butch Cassidy and the Sundance Kid* (1969). That film tweaked genre conventions enough to make the genre relevant, adding lighthearted humor and a contemporary soundtrack featuring the Oscar-winning tune "Raindrops Keep Fallin' on My Head" by Burt Bacharach and Hal David. In addition, John Wayne won his Best Actor Oscar for his role in *True Grit* (1969), a film and role that "summed up the Westerns of the past."[5] Future westerns like *The Wild Bunch* (1969) continued to push the genre, while others tried to capture its nostalgia, even more so showing *The Man Who Shot Liberty Valance* as the true end of an era. The classic era of westerns died with Liberty Valance, opening the door for an influx of genre evolution.

As we've seen, the film can also be viewed as a civil rights narrative of sorts. Johnson's original story was expanded in the early 1960s, when the news was full of debate over integration in the Jim Crow South. Front and center was the question of education. Pompey's desire to sit in Ranse's classroom and Tom's decision to pull Pompey away represents a dynamic push and pull of the 1960s political climate on race issues. A year after *The Man Who Shot Liberty Valance* comes out, a thousand minority kids marched in Birmingham, Alabama. Known as the Children's Crusade, this march against segregation was followed by Alabama governor George C. Wallace's standing in the way of two Black students trying to attend the University of Alabama. Later that year, Martin Luther King Jr. led his famous March on Washington for Jobs and Freedom. It is impossible to watch *The Man Who Shot Liberty Valance* without considering that it is a film about changing times released at a time of major change.

Westerns were waning throughout the 60s and 70s, despite some excellent additions to the canon. The year John Wayne died, 1979, Hollywood only made a handful of westerns. Pat Dowell, writing for the *Washington Post* in a 1980 feature titled "Back in the Saddle Again," wrote of the genre, "Perhaps the old warhorse is only being turned out to pasture—to be recalled to service at the last minute, just before the fadeout."[6] Dowell was writing of films like Walter Hill's *The Long Riders* (1980) and *Tom Horn* (1980), starring Steve McQueen. Of course, Michael Cimino's legendary box-office bomb *Heaven's Gate* (1980) would have a chilling effect on the genre for about a decade.

By the early 1990s, filmmakers were ready to test the western once again, proving that the genre did not ride off into the sunset like Alan Ladd in *Shane*. Best Picture Oscars for *Dances with Wolves* (1990) and *Unforgiven* (1992) during a lull in the genre "infected the town with Western fever," according to the *New York Times* in 1993.[7] CAA agent Robert Bookman told the *Times* that "*Unforgiven* made Westerns an acceptable genre again."[8] Films like *Tombstone, Wyatt Earp, City Slickers, The Quick and the Dead, Maverick, Posse,* and others graced the screen.

Producers always strike while the iron is hot, and whenever a western film or show scores a return on investment, there is sure to be imitators looking to cash in. Those who know the genre well will always be able to rise above any trendsetting and craft a narrative that connects the tumultuous Wild West to our current point in history.

CONTEMPORARY WESTERNS

Today, TV and streaming platforms lead the genre by driving it in new directions. Shows like *Deadwood*, *Justified*, and Taylor Sheridan's *Yellowstone*, whose season five premiere landed over twelve million viewers. The *Yellowstone* spinoffs *1883* and *1923*, known affectionately as part of the Taylor-verse, all hinge on the frontier thesis that has loomed large over the twentieth and twenty-first centuries. Sheridan's popular *Yellowstone* universe hits on the timeless binary conflicts inherent in the frontier mythos—wilderness vs. civilization, generational conflict, the treatment and displacement of Native Americans, and the many roles of women on the frontier.

The Duttons, *Yellowstone*'s protagonist family, are settlers of the frontier but also have the capacity to become one with it. John Dutton (Kevin Costner) shares a respectful rivalry with Chief Rainwater (Gil Birmingham); the two often seeking different ends while sharing appreciation for one another's traditions. *1883* introduces the family's admiration for Native Americans when Elsa Dutton (Isabel May) falls for a Native American and forces her family to consider changing their attitudes about the so-called savages. *1923* explicitly details the struggles of Native Americans in fascistic Catholic "re-education" camps.

More broadly, these shows remind us that while the frontier has long been settled, the debates and struggles it represents rage on. The role of women on the frontier, often relegated to homemaker or oldest profession status in the genre's earliest offerings, is not so limited in the Taylor-verse. The attitude of *Yellowstone*'s not-to-be-trifled-with Beth Dutton (Kelly Reilly) garners weekly commentary. *1923*'s Cara Dutton (Helen Mirren) is seen in the series opener chasing and blasting a shotgun at point-blank range at man who attacked her family. Mirren's character shows a combination of toughness and compassion that is unparalleled in the series. These popular characters track historically with Ford's frontier women, who are always strong.

Sheridan's stories also hinge on generational transitions. One coming to terms with their fate, another finding their place in the world. The Dutton sagas connect audiences to the allure of the frontier—its beauty and majesty—while challenging them to consider the cost of manifest destiny. These shows question popular legends about rugged individualism and examine the sexism, misogyny, and racism present in frontier narratives past and present. Parallel themes include loyalty, justice, tradition, courage, and a constant test of how far one will go to protect their family.

The western is arguably the most malleable genre, one that despite its usual setting in the late 1800s southwest remains remarkably timeless. The frontier, as a place and an idea, will always remain a canvas with endless possibilities. We can use it to confront the past or shape it to spark contemporary conversations. Perhaps no genre is better suited to confront societal change than the western, given how it is historically placed during a time of social and geographical upheaval. The renewed interest in frontier mythology will hopefully encourage some to take a trip back through the genre to see how the legacy of westerns is deeply rooted, both literally and figuratively, in confronting difficult terrain.

The Man Who Shot Liberty Valance continues to cast a long shadow over the genre with its timeless storytelling, moral ambiguity, and complex frontier themes still explored in contemporary westerns. The film managed to explore frontier justice, heroism, and the end of the Wild West in a beautiful and elegiac manner. As Richard Ray has written, "That Ranse's rise came at Tom's expense suggested the historical incompatibility of outlaw and official values."[9] Questions raised about the construction of legend remains timeless. The film's message translates into every changing era. The incompatibility of the past with the present creates constant friction that we grapple with as time evolves. As the clock ticks, we collectively decide what gets left behind and what gets brought with us into the future.

In many ways, *The Man Who Shot Liberty Valance* is a eulogy for time passed. This is one significant reason that the film has stayed with me. When I first saw the film as a teenager, it struck me as significant for reasons I couldn't quite understand beyond the passing of the Old West. As I write, I have now lived long enough to grieve for time past, though what I miss is quite different from that for which Ford yearned (Ford certainly would have grumbled over the 90s grunge and alternative music that I hold so dear). Similarities are found in how we grieve the high points of the past we've lived by engaging in art that represents what we miss. Processing his own thoughts on aging, Ford could relate more to Tom Doniphon but was smart enough to understand that Ranse Stoddard was the future.

Making meaning of our lives was also a central focus of Joseph Campbell's work on mythology, which can enrich not only how we see westerns but how we understand our own lives. The western is built on legends, just as the frontier itself was propelled by stories of a better life just over the next hill. *The Man Who Shot Liberty Valance* has it both ways, unveiling the facts while also printing the legend. Mythology puts us into relationship with our own world, and by offering both fact and fiction, *The Man Who Shot Liberty Valance* reminds us that when we look back, we must look closely. Enjoy the legends and stories, the film seems to say—they're fun, after all—but pay attention to the details of how our world's machinations.

When it comes to my own nostalgia, I just put on my turntable and share the music with my four-year-old daughter (you should see her dance to the Beastie Boys!). These experiences operate as a warm blanket of sorts, helping me see past, present, and future all at the same time, making peace with all three. *The Man Who Shot Liberty Valance* likely did this for Ford on some level, and its message can encourage us all to more meaningfully contemplate our lives.

NOTES

CHAPTER ONE

1. "Exhibitors Classify Films; Tell Which Bring Most Cash," *Exhibitors Herald*, July 9, 1927, 17, 43.

2. "Westerns on Way out as Public Taste Changes," *Motion Picture Herald*, April 1, 1933, 9.

3. Mae Tinee, "*Stagecoach* Is a Treat Loaded with Suspense," *Chicago Tribune*, February 25, 1939, 13.

4. Frank S. Nugent, "THE SCREEN: A Ford-Powered *Stagecoach* Opens at Music Hall," *New York Times*, March 3, 1939, 27.

5. Joseph W. Taylor, "Horse Operas Western Films Are Hollywood's Sure-Fire Financial Winners," *Wall Street Journal*, April 14, 1948, 1.

6. Ibid.

7. André Bazin, "The Evolution of the Western," in *The Western Reader*, ed. Jim Kitses and Gregg Rickman (Limelight Editions, 1998).

8. Ibid.

9. William R. Weaver, "The Top Money Making Stars of the Year Selected by Exhibitors," *Motion Picture Herald*, January 1, 1955, 13.

CHAPTER TWO

1. Frederick Jackson Turner, "The Significance of the Frontier in American History," in *The Frontier in American History* (Okitoks Press, 2017), 3.

2. Ibid.

3. Ibid., 7.

4. Ibid., 87.

5. Turner, 100.

6. Ibid., 13.

7. Clyde A. Millner, "Introduction: America, Only More So," in *The Oxford History of the American West*, ed. Clyde A. Milner II, Carol A. O'Connor, and Martha A. Sandweiss (Oxford University Press, 1994), 1.

8. Anne M. Butler, "Selling the Popular Myth," in *The Oxford History of the American West*, ed. Clyde A. Milner II, Carol A. O'Connor, and Martha A. Sandweiss (Oxford University Press, 1994), 772.

9. Ibid.

10. Dee Brown, *The American West* (Touchstone, 1994), 26.

11. Robert Warshow, "Movie Chronicle: The Westerner," in *The Western Reader*, ed. Jim Kitses and Gregg Rickman (Limelight, 1998), 35.

12. Portions of this section have been adapted from the author's master's thesis, "Printing the Legend: Western Influence on *The Shootist, Unforgiven, True Grit*, and *Zombieland*," Regent University, 2011.

13. Warshow, "Movie Chronicle," 38.

14. Ibid., 39.

15. Ibid.

16. Ibid., 47.

17. Ibid.

18. Thomas Schatz, "The Western," in *Hollywood Genres* (MacGraw-Hill, 1981), 77.

19. Ibid., 80.

20. Jim Kitses, *Horizons West: Directing the Western from John Ford to Clint Eastwood* (British Film Institute, 2004), 12.

21. Ibid., 13.

22. Ibid.

23. Richard B. Ray, *A Tendency of the Hollywood Cinema, 1930-1980* (Princeton University Press, 1985), 220.
24. Richard Slotkin, *Gunfighter Nation: The Myth of the Frontier in Twentieth-Century America*, (University of Oklahoma Press, 1998), 11.
25. Ibid., 492.
26. Jane Tompkins, *West of Everything: The Inner Life of Westerns* (Oxford University Press, 1992), 71.
27. Ibid., 72.
28. Michael Budd, "A Home in the Wilderness: Visual Imagery in John Ford's Westerns," in *The Western Reader*, ed. Jim Kitses and Gregg Rickman (Limelight, 1998), 134.
29. Kitses, *Horizons West*, 44.
30. Ibid., 30.

CHAPTER THREE

1. Gaylyn Studlar, "Sacred Duties, Poetic Passions: John Ford and the Issue of Femininity in the Western," in *John Ford Made Westerns*, ed. Gaylyn Studlar and Matthew Bernstein (Indiana University Press, 2001), 47.
2. Joan Didion, *Slouching Toward Bethlehem* (Farrar, Straus and Giroux, 2008), 30.
3. Ibid., 31.
4. Jane Tompkins, *West of Everything: The Inner Life of Westerns* (Oxford University Press, 1992), 3.
5. Ibid.
6. Ibid., 17.
7. Ibid.
8. Ibid., 50.
9. Ibid., 66.
10. Nancy Schoenberger, *Wayne and Ford: The Films, the Friendship, and the Forging of an American Hero* (Anchor, 2017), 127, 6.
11. Ibid., 127.
12. Molly Haskell, "What Makes John Wayne Larger than Life?," in *Holding My Own in No Man's Land* (Oxford University Press, 1997), 149.

13. Ibid.

14. Ibid., 151.

15. Ibid., 159.

16. Ibid., 152.

17. Ibid.

18. Schoenberger, *Wayne and Ford*, 5.

19. Ibid.

20. Steve Smith, *The Years and the Wind and the Rain: A Biography of Dorothy M. Johnson* (Pictorial Histories, 1984), x.

21. Ibid., 17.

22. Dorothy Johnson, "Some Lawmen I Have Known," *Montana: The Magazine of Western History* 25, no. 1 (Winter 1975): 55.

23. Ibid., 56.

24. Ibid., 59.

25. Ibid., 56.

26. Dorothy Johnson, *The Man Who Shot Liberty Valance and A Man Called Horse and The Hanging Tree and Los Sister: The Great Westerns of Dorothy M. Johnson* (River Bend, 2005). All quotations from Johnson's "The Man Who Shot Liberty Valance" are from this collection unless otherwise noted.

27. Joseph McBride and Michael Wilmington, *John Ford* (Da Capo, 1975), 188.

28. Joseph McBride, *Searching for John Ford* (University Press of Mississippi, 2011), 3.

29. Peter Bogdanovich, *Pieces of Time: Peter Bogdanovich on the Movies* (Arbor House/Esquire, 1973), 178.

30. Smith, *The Years and the Wind and the Rain*, 95.

31. Ibid.

32. Ibid., 196.

33. Lexy Perez and Trilby Beresford, "Jane Campion Fires back at Sam Elliott's *Power of the Dog* Criticism," *Hollywood Reporter*, March 15, 2022.

34. Ibid.

35. *Gravel in Her Gut and Spit in Her Eye*, dir. Bill Silverstone, PBS, 2005.

CHAPTER FOUR

1. Peter Bogdanovich, *Pieces of Time: Peter Bogdanovich on the Movie* (Arbor House/Esquire, 1973), 174.

2. William Kittredge and Steven M. Krauzer, eds., *Stories into Film* (Harper Colophon, 1979), 185.

3. Ibid., 186.

4. MPAA censorship records available at https://digitalcollections.oscars.org/digital/collection/p15759coll30/id/18875/rec/3.

5. Woody Strode, with Sam Young, *Goal Dust: An Autobiography by Woody Strode* (Madison Books, 1990), 205–6.

6. Ibid., 206.

7. Scott Eyman, *John Wayne: The Life and Legend* (Simon & Schuster, 2014), 360.

8. Bogdanovich, *Pieces of Time*, 140.

9. Joseph McBride, *Searching for John Ford* (University Press of Mississippi, 2011), 623.

CHAPTER FIVE

1. George L. Mitchell, "Ford on Ford," in *John Ford Interviews*, ed. Gerald Peary (University Press of Mississippi, 2001), 72.

2. Ibid.

3. "Only Top Quality Films in Paramount's Future," *BoxOffice*, October, 23, 1961, 11.

4. "Paramount Still in Picture Business," *Motion Picture Exhibitor*, June 14, 1961, 8.

5. Tag Gallagher, *John Ford: The Man and His Films* (University of California Press, 1986), 385.

6. Bill Libby, "The Old Wrangler Rides Again," in *John Ford Interviews* (University Press of Mississippi, 2001), 56.

7. Scott Eyman, *Print the Legend: The Life and Times of John Ford* (Simon & Schuster, 1999), 490.

8. Dan Ford, *Pappy: The Life of John Ford* (Prentice-Hall, 1979), 292.

9. Eyman, *Print the Legend*, 493.

10. Steven Bingen, with Marc Wanamaker, *Paramount: City of Dreams* (Taylor, 2017), 140.
11. Peter Bogdanovich, *Who the Hell's in It?* (Knopf, 2004), 291.
12. "150 Extras for Valance," *Hollywood Reporter*, October 20, 1961, 4.
13. Dwayne Epstein, *Lee Marvin: Point Blank* (Schaffner, 2013), 116.
14. Lee Marvin in conversation with Dan Ford, scene commentary, *The Man Who Shot Liberty Valance*, Blu-ray, 2022.
15. Nancy Schoenberger, *Wayne and Ford: The Films, the Friendship, and the Forging of an American Hero* (Anchor, 2017), 164.
16. Joseph McBride, *Searching for John Ford* (University Press of Mississippi, 2011), 630.
17. Epstein, *Lee Marvin*, 116.
18. Robert Ward, "The Story Behind Lee Marvin's Liberty Valance Smile," reprinted in *The Daily Beast*, April 14, 2017, www.thedailybeast.com.
19. Peter Bogdanovich, *Pieces of Time: Peter Bogdanovich on the Movies* (Arbor House/Esquire, 1973), 175. All quotations from this conversation are from this source unless otherwise noted.
20. Woody Strode, with Sam Young, *Goal Dust: An Autobiography by Woody Strode* (Madison Books, 1990), 210. All quotations from this conversation are from this source unless otherwise noted.
21. Ibid., 211.
22. Steven Bingen, Stephen X. Sylvester, and Michael Troyan, *MGM: Holly-wood's Greatest Backlot* (Santa Monica Press, 2011), 229.
23. Ibid., 228.
24. "Liberty Valance Goes on Location," *Hollywood Reporter*, October 26, 1961, 13. The web page of Conejo Valley, where Western film sets were regularly used, also has images from 1960–61. The web page also includes an image of an exterior of a barn that was possibly used in *The Man Who Shot Liberty Valance*; see www.conejovalleyguide.com.
25. A likely picture of the Tom Doniphon home can be found at www.venturaviews.com/GalleryMain.asp?GalleryID=169986&AKey=M235PYD5.
26. Woody Strode, with Sam Young, *Goal Dust: An Autobiography by Woody Strode* (Madison Books, 1990), 211.

27. Ibid., 212.

28. Jimmy Stewart in conversation with Dan Ford, scene commentary, *The Man Who Shot Liberty Valance*, Blu-ray, 2022.

29. Ibid.

30. Lee Marvin conversation with Dan Ford, scene commentary, *The Man Who Shot Liberty Valance*, Blu-ray, 2022.

31. Hedda Hopper, "Looking at Hollywood: Marvin Prefers Films' Artistic Freedom," *Chicago Daily Tribune*, December 5, 1961, B3.

32. Shooting schedule, page 11, John Ford Papers, Lilly Library.

33. 1st Preview notes, *The Man Who Shot Liberty Valance* file, John Ford Papers, Lily Library. All quotations are from this report until otherwise noted.

34. *The Man Who Shot Liberty Valance* file, John Ford Papers, Lily Library. All citations from foreign previews are from this file.

35. "Valance Music Promotion," *Hollywood Reporter*, April 16, 1962, 9.

CHAPTER SIX

1. Joseph McBride, *Searching for John Ford* (University Press of Mississippi, 2011), 623.

2. "The Man Who Shot Liberty Valance," *Harrison's Reports*, April 21, 1962, 58.

3. James Powers, "Liberty Valance Bang-Up Western for Hefty B.O.," *Hollywood Reporter*, April 11, 1962, 3. All reviews in this section are from the last cited source until otherwise noted.

4. "The Man Who Shot Liberty Valance," *Variety*, April 11, 1962, 6.

5. John L. Scott, "Liberty Valance Tale of Frontier Violence," *Los Angeles Times*, April 20, 1962, C10.

6. Tinee, Mae, "Film Offers Big Names, Tired Topic," *Chicago Daily Tribune*, April 27, 1962, B14.

7. "The Man Who Shot Liberty Valance," *Photoplay*, July 1962, 10.

8. "The Man Who Shot Liberty Valance," *New York Herald Tribune*, May 24, 1962, 15.

9. A. H. Weiler, "Man Who Shot Liberty Valance Opens at Capitol Theatre," *New York Times*, May 24, 1962, 29.

10. Hedda Hopper, "Ford Keeps ahead of Young Producers," *Los Angeles Times*, May 8, 1962, C14.
11. "Valance 30% Better Overseas than US-Canada," *Variety*, August 14, 1963, 12.
12. "Valance Big Abroad," *Hollywood Reporter*, November 16, 1963, 2.
13. Bill Libby, "The Old Wrangler Rides Again," in *John Ford Interviews* (University Press of Mississippi, 2001), 46–57. This interview is quoted at length, and the subsequent quotations are all form this interview until otherwise noted.
14. Bill Libby, "The Old Wrangler Rides Again," *Cosmopolitan* 156, no. 3, March 1964, 12–21.
15. Peter Bogdanovich, *John Ford* (University of California Press, 1978), 98–99.

CHAPTER SEVEN

1. André Bazin, "The Evolution of the Western," in *What Is Cinema*, vol. 2 (University of California Press, 1971), 149.
2. Ibid., 28.
3. Pauline Kael, "Circles and Squares," in *Auteurs and Authorship: A Film Reader*, ed. Barry Keith Grant (Blackwell, 2008), 51.
4. Ibid., 53.
5. Eric Leguèbe, "John Ford," in *John Ford Interviews* (University Press of Mississippi, 2001), 72.
6. Ibid., 73.
7. Axel Madsen, "Ford on Ford 1," in *John Ford Interviews* (University Press of Mississippi, 2001), 87.
8. Claudine Tavernier, "The Fourth Dimension of Old Age," in *John Ford Interviews* (University Press of Mississippi, 2001), 101.
9. Bertrand Tavernier, "Notes of a Press Attache: John Ford in Paris," in *John Ford Interviews*, (University Press of Mississippi, 2001), 108.
10. Evan Davis, "Peter Bogdanovich Shares His Memories of Orson Welles, and Who Really Deserves Credit for Citizen Kane," *Decider*, December 10, 2020.
11. Peter Wollen, "The Auteur Theory," in *Auteurs and Authorship: A Film Reader*, ed. Barry Keith Grant (Blackwell, 2008), 61.
12. Ibid.

13. Ibid., 62–63.

14. George Stevens Jr., *My Place in the Sun: Life in the Golden Age of Hollywood and Washington* (University Press of Kentucky, 2022), 284.

15. Ibid.

16. Peter Bogdanovich, *John Ford* (University of California Press, 1978), 109.

17. Ibid.

18. All the following quotations are from this broadcast unless otherwise noted. The historic broadcast is available on YouTube at www.youtube.com/watch?v=IddQiOCqZOM.

19. Bogdanovich, *John Ford*, 112.

20. Albin Krebs, "John Ford, the Movie Director Who Won 5 Oscars, Dies at 78," *New York Times*, September 1, 1973, 1.

CHAPTER EIGHT

1. Robert Warshow, "Movie Chronicle: The Westerner," in *The Western Reader*, ed. Jim Kitses and Gregg Rickman (Limelight Editions, 1998), 38.

2. Warshow, "Movie Chronicle," 47.

3. *Horizons West* was first published in 1969 and updated in 2004. For the purposes of clarity and concision, I will keep discussion of Kitses here instead of in multiple sections of this chapter, using only his chapter on John Ford.

4. Jim Kitses, *Horizons West* (BFI), 2004, 13.

5. Ibid., 42.

6. Kitses, *Horizons West*, 119.

7. Ibid., 121.

8. Ibid.

9. Ibid., 124.

10. Ibid., 125.

11. John G. Cawelti, *The Six-Gun Mystique Sequel* (Bowling Green State University Press, 1999), 32.

12. Ibid., 128.

13. Ibid., 141.

14. Ibid., 148.

15. Ibid.

16. Dan Ford, *Pappy: The Life of John Ford* (Prentice-Hall, 1979), 291.
17. Ibid., 293.
18. Dave Kehr, "The Man Who Shot Liberty Valance," *Chicago Reader*, January 17, 1986.
19. Tag Gallagher, *John Ford: The Man and His Films* (University of California Press, 1986), 385.
20. Gallagher, *John Ford*, 385.
21. Scott Eyman, *Print the Legend: The Life and Times of John Ford* (Simon & Schuster, 1999), 492.
22. Ibid., 360.
23. Joseph McBride, *Searching for John Ford* (University Press of Mississippi, 2011), 626.
24. Ibid., 628.
25. Ibid., 632.
26. Joseph McBride and Michael Wilmington, *John Ford* (Da Capo, 1975), 181.
27. Charles J. Maland, "From Aesthete to Pappy: The Evolution of John Ford's Public Reputation," in *John Ford Made Westerns: Filming the Legend in the Sound Era*, ed. Gaylyn Studlar and Matthew Bernstein (Indiana University Press, 2001), 242.
28. Ibid., 242.
29. David Lusted, *The Western* (BFI, 2003), 213.
30. Patrick McGee, *From Shane to Kill Bill: Rethinking the Western* (Blackwell, 2007), 135.
31. Ibid., 137.
32. Richard Brody, "The Man Who Shot Liberty Valance," *New Yorker*, October 21, 2009. www.newyorker.com.
33. Roger Ebert, "The Western Frontier, between Fact and Legend," Roger Ebert.com, December 28, 2011, www.rogerebert.com.
34. Ibid.
35. Abigail Horne, "The Color of Manhood: Reconsidering Pompey in *John Ford's The Man Who Shot Liberty Valance*," in *Black Camera* 4, no. 1 (Winder 2012): 21.
36. Ibid., 10.

37. Sue Matheson, *The Westerns and War Films of John Ford* (Rowman & Littlefield, 2016), xvii.
38. Ibid., 260.
39. Nancy Schoenberger, *Wayne and Ford: The Films, the Friendship, and the Forging of an American Hero* (Anchor, 2017), 167.
40. Ibid., 171.
41. Oliver Macnaughton, "The Man Who Shot Liberty Valance at 60: The Great American Western," *Guardian*, April 22, 2022, www.theguardian.com/.
42. Ibid.

CHAPTER NINE

1. Joseph Campbell, *Pathways to Bliss: Mythology and Personal Transformation* (New World Library, 2004), xvi.
2. Christopher Vogler, *The Writer's Journey: Mythic Structure for Writers* (Michael Wiese Productions, 2007), xiii.
3. Joseph Campbell, *The Hero with a Thousand Faces* (Pantheon, 1949; repr., New World Library, 2008), 14.
4. Ibid.
5. Ibid., 15.
6. Stuart Voytilla, *Myth and the Movies: Discovering the Mythic Structure of 50 Unforgettable Films* (Michael Wise, 1999), 48.
7. Campbell, *The Hero with a Thousand Faces*, 7.
8. The actual 1865 quote, assumed to be from Greely, is "Washington is not a place to live in. The rents are high, the food is bad, the dust is disgusting, and the morals are deplorable. Go West, young man, go West and grow up with the country."
9. Campbell, *The Hero with a Thousand Faces*, 84.
10. Campbell, *Pathways to Bliss*, 133.
11. Campbell, *The Hero with a Thousand Faces*, 306.
12. Ibid., 307.
13. Campbell, *Pathways to Bliss*, 132.

CHAPTER TEN

Portions of this chapter are adapted from a column I published in *The Hollywood Reporter* titled "What Studio Franchises Can Learn from the Rise, Fall, and Rise of the Western," March 21, 2023.

1. Joseph Campbell, *Pathways to Bliss: Mythology and Personal Transformation* (New World Library, 2004), xv.

2. References to Andrew Nelson in this chapter are based on personal conversations with the author.

3. Frederick Jackson Turner, "The Significance of the Frontier in American History," 3. A full text of speech can be found at www.usmcu.edu/Portals/218/Turner%20Thesis%2C%20Frederick%20Jackson%20Turner.pdf.

4. Campbell, *Pathways to Bliss*, xvi.

5. Paul Monaco, *The Sixties: 1960–1969* (University of California Press, 2001), 180.

6. Pat Dowell, "Back in the Saddle Again: Hollywood's $100-Million Stampede to Bring back the Western," *Washington Post*, May 11, 1980, H1.

7. Bernard Weiraub, "Hollywood Recycles the Western to Offer New Heroes: Women," *New York Times*, May 3, 1993, C11.

8. Ibid.

9. Richard Ray, *A Certain Tendency in Hollywood Cinema, 1930–1980*, (Princeton University Press, 1985), 329.